A Place of Refuge

"I've been impressed with the emotional depth of Asmaa's writing for a while now. Her words make you just stop and feel. This work of hers is no different. Thank you, Asmaa."

— **Sh Muhammad AlShareef,**
Founder and Director of DiscoverU Life

"Rare is a reading experience that touches your soul, heart and mind equally. *A Place of Refuge* grants us such an experience. Asmaa Hussein weds deep spiritual insights with everyday encounters, as well as the legacy of painful traumas—both of which are equally accessible to all readers due to the evocative use of sparse and clear prose—and we are left with this moving truth: our connection to our Sustainer is the undercurrent that carries us to our place of loving refuge again and again. There wasn't a single essay that didn't bring me to tears with this truth. Stunning in its impact, this is a must-read for all human hearts."

— **S.K. Ali,** *award-winning and New York Times bestselling author of Love from A to Z and The Proudest Blue*

"This is a moving testament to love and commitment, and through it I have no doubt that many others will find much to share, appreciate and admire. As well, it demonstrates the infinite power of faith in healing emotional wounds and dealing with psychological trauma."

— **Dr. Yasir Qadhi,** *Dean of Academic Affairs, The Islamic Seminary of America*

"*A Place of Refuge* by Asmaa Hussein is an honest and frank conversation about what grieving loss actually looks like. It is real. It will take you through an emotional roller coaster ranging from extreme discomfort to a big smile because you can deeply relate to what she is talking about. We often don't know why we go through the challenges and trials that we do. However, one thing I took away from this book is that pain is a powerful way to establish common grounds with people and develop true relationships. Perhaps it is one of the wisdoms behind the Prophet being described as: 'There has certainly come to you a Messenger from among yourselves. Grievous to him is what you suffer...' I would highly recommend this book to everyone looking for help navigating through difficult emotions, particularly relating to grief and loss."

— **Sh Navaid Aziz,** *Instructor at AlMahgrib Institute*

"*A Place of Refuge* is a beautifully written book filled with parables about modern life. It is a book about pain, grief, and self-doubt, but also one about faith, trust, hope, and happiness. Asmaa Hussein uses deeply personal events to weave broad lessons for anyone going through the toils of life. Muslim readers will find special significance in Qur'anic verses and Prophetic traditions they have heard and read many times before, but which the book effectively connects to raw, lived human experience. This is an emotional, difficult book, but one which will prove important for contemporary Muslims searching for greater spiritual meaning and purpose."

— **Mohamad Hamas Elmasry,**
Associate Professor of Media and Cultural Studies,
Doha Institute for Graduate Studies

"Within pages of reading Asmaa's book, I put it down for a moment to recalibrate because of intensity of the raw emotion I didn't even know I needed to feel. Throughout her book, her words brought me to tears in awe of Allah, drove me to make *du'a*, and rekindled a deep awareness that Allah truly only plans what is best for us."

— **Maryam Amir**

A Place of
Refuge

ASMAA HUSSEIN

A Place of Refuge

Published by:
Ruqaya's Bookshelf
Toronto, Ontario, Canada
www.ruqayasbookshelf.com
ISBN: 978-1-989079-13-3

Cover design by Identify BDA
Edited by Hajera Khaja
Copy edited by Amina Sadler
Typesetting by Identify BDA

Printed and bound in China

In the name of Allah, the Most Beneficent,
the Most Merciful

For Amr and Ruqaya

If our words of prayer could be seen,
what would they look like?

I'd like to imagine they'd be like butterflies:
weightless, ethereal beings
fluttering about in the clouds,
being lifted up, up, up to God.

I wish I could see them floating out of windows,
slipping out through prison bars,
rising from people's tongues and chests.

I wish I could see them swarm the sky.

Contents

Note to the Reader

- Arabic words and phrases appear in italics in the text. Definitions can be found in the glossary at the end of the book.

- The translations of the meanings of the verses of the Qur'an in this book are taken, with some minor changes, from *The Qur'an: Arabic Text with Corresponding English Meanings* by Saheeh International.

Abbreviations for honourifics appearing in this book:

- (swt): *subhanahu wa ta'ala:* the Exalted; used with the name of Allah

- (saw): *salla Allahu 'alayhi wa sallam:* may the peace and blessings of Allah be upon him; used with the name of Prophet Muhammad

- (as): *'alayhi / 'alayha salam:* peace be upon him/her; used after the names of prophets and others

- (ra): *radi Allahu 'anhu / 'anha:* may Allah be pleased with him/her; used after the name of a Companion of the Prophet

A Place of
Refuge

I am here

The dreaded middle seat. I sat stiffly on my plane ride into Jeddah, arms glued to my sides. If I leaned a centimeter too far right or left, I'd be rubbing shoulders with either an old Palestinian woman or a young Nigerian man.

The irony of my caution, of course, would become apparent when I made my first ever *tawaf* and realized it was impossible not to rub shoulders with countless pilgrims, both men and women, performing the same act of worship.

For the first time in my life, I was going to Makkah. I would tare the *Ka'bah* I had been facing in prayer my whole life. I would walk on the same ground as our Messenger (saw) and his Companions. I would witness the place in which the roots of our faith first took hold—with Ibrahim,

Ismail, and Hajar, then with Prophet Muhammad (peace and blessings upon them all).

As we got closer to our arrival in Jeddah, our group leader stood up on the plane and instructed us to verbalize our intention to perform *'umrah* before passing the *meeqat*. Once the intention had been spoken, we would officially be in a state of *ihram*.

I whispered the intention to myself: *Labayk Allahumma 'umrah* (O Allah, I intend to perform *'umrah*). My hajj intention would be stated at a later time.

Once we had passed over the *meeqat*, the voices of hundreds of men and women, from so many different countries around the world, began chanting the same *talbiyah*. The airplane resonated with their beautiful words: *Here I am, O Allah, here I am. Here I am, You have no partner, here I am. Surely all praise, favour, and authority belong to You. You have no partner.*

I quietly recited with them, absorbed in my own thoughts.

I had received my hajj visa mere days before my travel date. Up until then, I wasn't sure if my incomplete documents were sufficient for a visa. My hajj group said they'd try their best to push my application through, but there was no guarantee I'd make the cut. It was at the discretion of the Saudi Arabian embassy.

I spent weeks impatiently waiting to hear the news. I obsessively checked my phone for e-mail notifications. I typed impatient follow-up messages to the group organizers, only to delete them before sending them. I kept myself occupied with whatever writing and editing work I could get my hands on.

I packed my suitcase halfheartedly, knowing full well that my visa might not be issued at all. Would I use the unscented soaps and shampoos I had bought for when I would be in a state of *ihram*? Would I get the chance to wear the light cotton *abayas* I had gotten sewn by a local seamstress? What would happen to the Costco-sized box of energy bars or pack of electrolyte tablets I bought to stay energized and hydrated in the Makkah heat? I folded and sorted and stuffed them all into my one suitcase, all while not knowing the answer.

I asked Allah (swt) to make it easy and facilitate this journey, all the while mentally preparing myself to face disappointment if I didn't end up travelling.

About a week before the travel date, I had just finished praying *fajr*. I was still sitting on my prayer mat when I heard the familiar 'ping' of my phone. A message. I reached for my phone and saw a one-line message from a group organizer:

Your du'as have been answered. Your hajj visa has been issued. Mabrook!

It was really happening. I immediately fell into a prostration of gratitude to Allah (swt).

For a long time before this moment I had raised my hands to Allah (swt), asking Him for the opportunity to visit the blessed cities of Makkah and

Madinah. At twenty-seven years old, I had suddenly been widowed. Emerging from that pain felt nearly impossible at the time. I believed that performing hajj might be a part of my healing process.

Years had passed since then, though, and I witnessed so many friends and family members make the journey while I remained at home.

Going for hajj felt so out of reach that it eventually fell off my radar. I hadn't made *du'a* for it for a very, very long time. But for reasons beyond my knowledge, Allah (swt) had destined this 2019 hajj for me. He never forgot my desire to visit the holy cities, even though that yearning within me had been muted by the noise of life. He never forgot the words I uttered into my open palms in the middle of my most difficult moments of grief.

{…And never is your Lord forgetful.} *(Maryam 19: 64)*

When I finally received my passport with the visa attached to the back cover, I stared hard at it for a minute or two. I ran my hand over the adhesive square sheet that had my photo and personal information typed on it. *Issued by the Saudi mission in Ottawa*, it said at the top. This was it. This would grant me entry into Saudi Arabia.

What once felt impossible, Allah had made easy.

As I sat and recited the *talbiyah* on the airplane, I couldn't help but be amazed that Allah (swt) had brought me here. My voice was united in recitation with people from across the globe, all of them travelling to this blessed land for the same reason as me. Every one of us was chosen by Him to make this journey at this particular time.

My statement to God, *I am here*, was so simple, yet I was aware that it held the apex of my very purpose of existing.

I left everything behind so that I could come here. I pressed 'pause' on my business. I paid off my outstanding debts. I wrote a document for my family with all my e-mail and bank account passwords. I wrote my will. I left my sweet six-year-old daughter with my family. I hugged her tight before I left and whispered into her ear, "I'll see you soon, *in sha' Allah*."

Then I walked out of my normal life, saying to Allah: *Here I am*.

Here I am, leaving behind all the blessings that I enjoy and love to serve You and to acknowledge your Oneness, to fulfill the pillar of hajj as You have commanded of me.

Here I am, not knowing if I will return to my business, my wealth, my family, or my child, who is dearer to me than my own self.

Here I am, acknowledging that everything in this world will be left behind when my soul is taken and it rises to meet You.

Here I am, without anything or anyone to hide behind, baring my troubled and sinful soul to You, the Most Forgiving.

I cried in the midst of reciting these words. Before

this, I had written so many articles and social media posts about prioritizing the worship of God above all else. But in this singular moment, and perhaps for the first time ever, I finally understood what it meant to shed the *dunya* in favour of the hereafter.

Every person on that airplane, and every one of the millions of people who came for hajj, left something or someone they loved behind. Their journeys were made in anticipation of receiving something better and more beloved: Allah's forgiveness and acceptance.

In the years that led up to this moment, friends and loved ones (and sometimes even strangers) would consistently say to me, "Allah will replace what you lost with something better."

They were referring to the verse in which Allah (swt) promises:

{...If Allah knows [any] good in your hearts, He will give you [something] better than what was taken from you, and He will forgive you; and Allah is Forgiving and Merciful.} *(al-Anfal 8: 70)*

Although the statement is absolutely beautiful, whenever I heard or read it, I would flinch because I knew it was being said to me specifically in the context of finding a new husband after my Amr passed away. I didn't want to hear it.

I didn't want to hear that my husband, to whom I had gifted all my love, was going to be replaced by someone "better." It made my heart hurt. It even made me angry.

The worst part is that I began to dislike hearing the statement. I would gloss over it whenever I read it—not because I didn't believe it, but because it was so often used to nudge me towards a path I wasn't ready to take.

Sitting on that airplane to Jeddah, I looked back on the past few years of my life and took stock of all the incredible things that had happened to me. I had started a publishing company from scratch. My books were in thousands of homes throughout the world. I had travelled across North America to give speeches and meet my readers. I had been given the strength and patience to raise an incredibly energetic and opinionated child on my own.

In the midst of tending to my broken heart and walking in the shadow of my grief, Allah (swt) was quietly replacing what I had lost with something better. He was giving me the opportunity to live for a greater purpose than just my own life. He was showing me how to turn to Him in my brokenness and find gratitude even in pain.

As though it were a culmination of all the blessings I had experienced, I was now on my way to perform hajj. What I wanted most was simply to lay my eyes on the *Ka'bah*: the structure I faced whenever I raised my hands to God in moments of great loneliness. I wanted to feel like I was more than just an individual wandering this life alone. I wanted to feel like I was a part of innumerable generations of believers who had come here to declare their worship of and belief in One God.

On that airplane, I reclaimed the statement, *Allah will replace what you lost with something better*, because I saw how it manifested itself so beautifully in my life, even without my husband being physically "replaced."

When Allah (swt) promises to replace what we lose with what is better, the breadth and richness of that promise is so much greater than what we can imagine. Yes, He may replace our losses with tangible, material things or people. But He might also replace our losses with a desire to be close to Him, to leave a greater legacy behind, to gather people and encourage them on this path of worship.

If we are among the few who are grateful to Allah (swt) and who worship Him regardless of circumstance, then He has already replaced anything we could possibly lose with something better. May Allah make us amongst those few.[1]

When the plane finally landed, we all stepped out into the dry Jeddah heat. Eager pilgrims rushed about, yelling instructions to their travel groups and then clamouring past one another for spots on the buses to the terminal.

In the middle of the swarm of people around me, I was quiet and my heart focused. I was already thinking of what was to come.

I am here, I whispered to Allah (swt) on that tarmac. *I am here, and I am ready for the beautiful things that are about to come my way, by Your will.*

Thrive in grief

In Makkah, my ears picked up the familiar dialect of Egyptians who had come for hajj. They littered their sentences with hard "g"s instead of "j"s. In every prayer line, every hotel lobby, and every grocery store, I would inadvertently listen in on their conversations. They talked about what anyone else would talk about: the heat, the crowd, the prices of groceries. But I couldn't stop listening.

Their sun-creased, bronzed faces made me nostalgic for the days I had spent in Egypt with my husband. The intense heat and scent of hot asphalt burning in Makkah's sun would suddenly tug at loose strings of memories I thought I had tied up and tucked away.

I remembered walking hand-in-hand with Amr along the streets of Alexandria in the evening. I'd listen to the playfulness of the Egyptian dialect bouncing off the pothole-riddled pavement. The car horns and the chatter would merge into a comforting hum. The smell of Alexandria—heavy smoke mixed with sticky ocean breeze—clung to my every sense.

I haven't set foot in the country since 2013, and I live nine thousand kilometers away. Still, after all these years, it was as though I were there again.

In the same Alexandria that tour guides and travel agencies laud as stunning, breathtaking, and full of unforgettable historical sights, much of the woman I used to be was erased and much of who I am now was born.

While we were on vacation in the summer of 2013, my husband, Amr, marched in protest of the massacre of Egyptians at the hands of the military following the coup d'état. He was shot and killed by an Egyptian army sniper on August 16 of that year.

"I'm not ready for this," I repeated under my breath, over and over, just after getting the call that my husband had been shot and killed. Someone had taken hold of Amr's phone and called the last dialed number. It just happened to be mine.

"I'm not ready for this. Please. I'm not ready for this," I said to God as I pawed through my drawers, trying to find an *abaya* to put on.

As I put on the black *abaya* I had found stuffed into one of my drawers, a feeling of unyielding dread sat like a hot stone in my belly. I hoped, against my own intuition, that the person who called me had made a mistake. *Maybe it wasn't Amr*, I thought. *Maybe it's someone else who was shot. Maybe Amr just lost his phone and someone is playing a cruel trick on me.*

Right after that phone call, Amr's dad had gotten up and rushed out of the house. The rest of us couldn't do anything except wait for news.

For half an hour I clung to a sliver of hope that this was all some kind of misunderstanding. I paced back and forth in the house. I tried contacting some of my husband's friends to see if they were with him. I looked up at the sky, pleading with God to wake me up from what felt like a horrific nightmare.

But soon after, we got the confirmation call from Amr's dad. He found Amr's body, bloody and lifeless, in a nearby *masjid* where fellow protesters had carried him. Amr's glasses were gone, perhaps knocked off his face when he was shot through his chin and he fell to the earth. I still wonder about his glasses sometimes. Where did they end up?

I told God that day, as my forehead was pressed to the ground: *I am not ready to be a widow after less than three years of marriage. I am not ready to be a single mother just nine months after having a baby. I am not ready to be alone after having searched so long for a loving partner with whom to share this life.*

I was beyond certain that I wouldn't be able to

bear this. It was unfathomable to me that I could continue existing after having said goodbye to my husband as his body lay in the hospital morgue. It felt impossible that I could watch my baby grow into a beautiful girl without her father by her side.

I was so sure I wasn't strong enough for this.

Grief. It first came at me like a rage-filled hurricane. It tore apart whatever joys I had built in this world. It forced me to hide away, to take cover lest it destroy me along with everything else in its path.

And hide away I did, writing and interacting with the world mostly from a small, dark room as my daughter slept. The more I published about my journey on social media, the bigger my online presence became. Yet the online world seemed so distant from my actual life.

In the real world, I made myself as physically small as I could. I kept away from Islamic events and even my friends' gatherings. I donated half my wardrobe because I just didn't care about my appearance anymore. I didn't plan what I'd do in a year or two. I just woke up every day and mechanically did the day's deeds. I was tethered to reality only by the movement of the sun and moon that were simply adhering to their orbits.

I lived in that bubble for a long time, comforted by its smallness and by the distance it put between me and having to face the real world.

As the years passed and I slowly emerged from that self-made storm shelter, I saw that the landscape of my life had drastically changed. The storm had uprooted and scattered so much of what I had carefully watered and tended to.

I had lost old friends who couldn't meet me where I was in my grief, who were too uncomfortable admitting they couldn't sit with my pain.

I noticed parts of my life, and parts of *me*, were just gone. My sense of humour had changed. I had always been a "make-everything-into-a-joke" kind of person, but that wasn't me anymore.

I began to be triggered by seemingly innocuous things like the news that my sister would be moving an hour outside of Toronto. It devastated me, even though I'd still see her regularly. When friends told me they were getting married or expecting a child, I would spiral into an unfamiliar internal darkness. *Everyone is moving forward, and I'm stuck.*

I didn't recognize this version of myself. I didn't like her. When I looked in the mirror, I saw something alien inhabiting my body.

To an outsider it may make logical sense that as time passes, grief is slowly forgotten and buried away, and things go back to the way they were.

The truth, though, is that my grief transformed as time passed. Some of it evaporated, yes, and that is a result of the great and unmatched mercy of God. But some of it remained, taking on a new shape inside my skin: nonspecific anger that seeped into all my interactions, fear of being abandoned by others whom I loved, and the emotional detachment that was eventually grown from those seeds.

I have lived an abundance of low points, cradling my brokenness in my hands, struggling with the new, ever-transforming faces of my grief. I have certainly wrestled with patience, trying so hard to hold on to it only to have it slip away from me again and again.

But each day that I get out of bed, try again, and slowly walk forward negates the statement I made all those years ago: "I'm not ready for this." I thought I wasn't ready, but the time that passed has said to me: *You are ready for this. You always have been.*

My life has been a testament to the *ayah* in which Allah (swt) reassures us:

{Allah does not burden a soul beyond what it can bear...} *(al-Baqarah 2: 286)*

Allah (swt) promises this strength to us. There is no tragedy, no pain, and no burden given to us that is too much. No matter what it is, we have the ability to withstand it, even though it may feel like it will swallow us whole.

Although the grief has permanently transformed me, I found within its layers new ways of looking at the world. A roadblock now looked like an opportunity for patience. Sadness was now a doorway that could lead to seeking comfort in the remembrance of Allah (swt). Darkness became a rite of passage on the journey back into the light.

I discovered an inner strength I didn't know I possessed—a strength that hadn't surfaced until I needed it. It was like a dormant creature, building its massive armour and power through faith and worship, just waiting to be called to arms by the difficulties that invaded my life. It came and pressed its fingers into my shoulder as I stood over my husband's body and said my final goodbyes. It surrounded me as I boarded a plane and flew away from the place he was taken, holding me steady in the air until I arrived into the arms of my family. It gripped my hands and pulled me forward when all I wanted to do was stand still and be broken.

When I felt that strength weakening, I held on to it by doing what gave it life to begin with: turning to Allah (swt) in *du'a*, reading and listening to the Qur'an, and taking time to reflect on and appreciate my surroundings. I made my movements slow; I would look out the window of my room, searching for the moon in all its stages. I prayed with the curtain open so it would cast light on the prayer mat in front of me. It reminded me that there would always be a ray of light to pierce the darkness, and there would always be hope descending from the skies.

We all have the strength to find people to help us and the ability to use the pain to grasp more tightly to His rope. It's often the great depths of pain that push us to surrender our will and our hearts to the Controller of all our affairs.

Because I have written about grief extensively, people around the world open up to me when they've lost their spouses, their children, or their parents. Their messages all express the same pain: *I can't see a way out of this pit of infinite sadness.*

We never invite heartbreak into our lives. It is a forever-unwelcome guest. We don't want it to come in and touch our things. When it knocks on our door, we pretend we're not home. We might drown out the knocking with unending text conversations and a steady stream of loud TV shows. We do whatever it takes to not let it in.

But one way or another, despite our best attempts to keep heartbreak away, it enters and makes itself comfortable.

Every person will eventually experience the loss of a loved one, and this is why I'm often asked by my readers, my friends, and even conference organizers to address the question, "How does one overcome grief?"

I hear the notes of desperation behind this question. I hear the desire in their voices and words to understand how to stitch up these dark, gaping wounds in their hearts.

Whether I am standing at a podium or sitting in front of my laptop, I dutifully and automatically respond with prepared bullet points:

Practice patience, connect to the Qur'an, make du'a, have faithful friends who remind you of God.

It's a beautiful answer, and it's true that all these things bring comfort to the grieving heart. But it's still not the *right* answer. There is no right answer because the question, "How does one overcome grief?" is fundamentally flawed.

In asking it, we are trying to find the formula to live a life free of a terrible, agonizing sadness, grief, or anger. These feelings are uncomfortable, so we want to know how we can get rid of them.

The short answer is: *We can't.*

I will always live with the memory of seeing my husband in that morgue. My heart cannot forget how it felt to look into my daughter's eyes, knowing what she didn't know yet—that her father was gone. Periodically, scents and sounds and familiar phrases inadvertently trigger my memories and transport me right back to some of my most painful moments.

These are not things I can simply get rid of or overcome.

I often remember the pain of Prophet Ya'qoub when he was separated from his son, Yusuf. Some scholars say that their separation lasted forty years, until Ya'qoub had gone blind with grief. Later in the story, when his other sons returned from Egypt after being in the presence of Yusuf, their father said to them:

21

{...Indeed, I detect the smell of Yusuf.} *(Yusuf 12: 94)*

When Ya'qoub mentioned the scent of Yusuf, his sons responded to him:

{...By Allah, indeed you are in your [same] old error.} *(Yusuf 12: 95)*

They responded the same way many people in our communities *still* respond to those who are grieving: *Stop bringing it up. Can't you just get over it? Patience means not being sad!*

But Prophet Ya'qoub was not sinful for grieving or feeling pain. Nor are we. For forty years he grieved, for forty years he held on to hope, and for forty years he couldn't forget the smell of his son. It's a pain that's so real and palpable that our hearts can't help but connect to it.

Many of those around me still don't understand the depth and transformative nature of grief. They tell me to stop writing about my husband. They say, *That's enough now.* Even as early as mere weeks after his passing, well-meaning people offhandedly stated, *Don't worry. You'll find someone else to marry instead of Amr.*

Within these words spoken or written to me, I heard the misguided assumption that there must be an expiration date on my pain. But that date does not exist.

The most recent "advice" shared with me online was: "The only way to stop pain in your life is to accept that nothing is yours. Everything is given to you by God, and everything will return to Him."

This statement is just one of many similar ones I've heard and read, so it felt familiar. It proposes that as humans, we have the power to stop feeling pain if only we believed in God *deeply enough*.

I had unknowingly internalized this belief from years of listening to and reading Islamic content that proposed the same. I had to forcefully unlearn it when I was faced with the death of my husband. I had to make a choice either to believe I was a bad Muslim because I was grieving so deeply, or believe in the utter falseness of statements that absurdly announced that having patience and faith meant leading a painless life.

Allah (swt) tells us that He's going to test us with fear, hunger, and loss of wealth and lives and resources. We are told outright: difficult and painful things are coming your way, so be ready to respond with:

{...Verily to Allah we belong, and to Him we shall return. Those are the people who are given glad tidings and mercy from Allah...} *(al-Baqarah 2: 156-157)*

Saying and believing that everything and everyone belongs to Allah (swt) doesn't mean we aren't going to grieve our losses, though. Rather, the people who are able to grieve and still maintain their faith are those who have truly understood and accepted their God-given humanity.

Allah (swt) created us with the capacity to feel

overwhelming joy, excitement, pain, sadness, anger, and every other sensation on the spectrum of emotions. These emotions are not a problem in and of themselves. In fact, the emotions we experience can push us to worship Allah (swt) more holistically and sincerely.

That being said, knowing our emotions are natural shouldn't make us resign ourselves to living in the shadow of pain. Sadness is lifted by Allah's will. Joy is reinstated, and ease always comes with difficulty.

We don't choose what tests come our way. Allah (swt) chooses. Our tests come in waves—sometimes gently, coaxing us towards remembrance; sometimes with so much force that we're nearly knocked to the ground. We will inhabit pockets of grief and stress many, many times in our lives.

Instead of constantly trying to overcome pain, what if we accepted every emotion that came our way? What if we stopped asking, "How does one overcome grief?" and instead asked, "How does one grow and thrive in grief?"

Prophet Muhammad (saw) said:

"How wonderful is the affair of the believer, for his affairs are all good, and this applies to no one but the believer. If something good happens to him, he is thankful for it and that is good for him. If something bad happens to him, he bears it with patience and that is good for him."[2]

Every test, every pang of sorrow, every moment

of joy, and every spot of disappointment is good for you if you know how to use it and how to thrive in it. What's important is how we use our circumstances and our emotions to fulfill our ultimate purpose, which is the worship of Allah.

In my pain, I did many things I would only later realize were attributes of growing and thriving. I wrote ferociously and without pause, relieving the ever-rising emotional pressure in my chest. I stopped attributing joy and meaning to material possessions, which helped me be more liberal with my charitable donations. I read the Qur'an from cover to cover, again and again, until my previously choppy recitation became smooth and easy.

None of these actions made me feel like I was thriving. I actually felt like I was always on the brink of drowning, barely surviving at all. In retrospect, however, I can see that they allowed me to manage my pain and to use it as a springboard towards something greater than just myself. I did these things because I understood at that point in my life, perhaps better than I understand even now, that this world is temporary. Wealth and material things come and go, our very existence is fleeting, and the deeds we send forward are all that will remain. I was acutely aware that my heartbreak would be lifted the moment I stepped foot into the paradise of eternity, *in sha' Allah*.

{And they will say, "Praise to Allah, who has removed from us [all] sorrow. Indeed, our Lord is

Forgiving and Appreciative..."} *(Fatir 35: 34)*

Perhaps our hearts will be more at ease when we accept that we're not trying to overcome anything. We're trying to grow and thrive, not only *despite* our pain, but *within* it as well.

The grief that began as a hot stone sizzling in my belly has been whittled away into a small bead that I now carry around my neck. It's true that this bead goes wherever I go, but that's not really the point.

The point is: *I go.*

Farah and Atta

On Friday, August 16, 2019, I was in Madinah. After 'asr prayer, I separated from my hajj group and went to sit by myself in Al-Masjid Al-Nabawi.

It was the sixth anniversary of my husband's death.

Amr passed away on a Friday around the time of 'asr, and it had taken six years for the anniversary to land on a Friday again.

This year, I was fortunate enough to be in one of the most blessed places, on the most blessed day of the week, in the hour about which the Prophet (saw) told us:

"On Friday there is an hour when, if a Muslim happens to pray at that time and ask Allah for something good, He will give it to him."[3]

I found a quiet spot by one of the marble

pillars in the women's section. I took out my small notebook of handwritten *du'as* I had brought with me from Canada, and raised my hands to ask for forgiveness and mercy for Amr. I asked Allah (swt) to raise his rank in paradise, to grant him the status of a martyr, and to take care of our daughter and me in his absence.

Despite being in this blessed place, with thousands of worshippers around me, I felt profoundly alone.

Although people who have followed my story know that I often write about how I grapple with grief, I am still a very private person. I will not interrupt someone's joy or laughter with my grief. I will not force it upon anyone, nor will I bring it into conversation unless I'm specifically asked about it. Naturally then, I didn't tell anyone in my hajj group about the significance of that day.

Every August 16 of every year that has passed since Amr's death has been difficult. It makes me count all the things that have happened since Amr has been gone—our daughter's milestones that we could have marked together, the victories in my business that we could have celebrated as a family, and the many setbacks that we could have overcome as husband and wife.

Every August 16, I involuntarily rummage through my memories until I'm back to the moment when I found out my life had changed forever.

In the midst of my *du'a* in Al-Masjid Al-Nabawi, I received a text message from my friend, Farah, with whom I had been trying to connect for several days. She was also performing hajj this year. We tried to meet in Makkah, but it was too busy and chaotic. She was in Madinah now, just for another day, and we were trying to make the meeting happen.

I'm at the masjid *now. Can you meet me outside door 25 after* maghrib?

Yes, she replied. She would.

I had never met Farah in person. We got in touch after her husband, Atta Elayyan, was killed on March 15, 2019 in the Christchurch, New Zealand massacre, when a violent white nationalist had gunned down fifty-one Muslims during Friday prayer.

Before we ever spoke, it was her photo with her husband and baby girl, Aya, that gave me the greatest pause when looking at all the victims' photos. She reminded me of myself. Atta reminded me of Amr. Aya reminded me of Ruqaya. My heart was overwhelmed because I knew that her daughter would grow up without her dad, like my Ruqaya. I knew what was coming for them—the days, months, and years of pain, questions, and anger.

It wasn't by chance that she found me on social media. It was all part of Allah's plan, and it was leading up to this very moment in Madinah.

Farah texted me saying she was wearing purple. I scanned the crowd as I exited the *masjid* after prayer. I finally saw her walking towards me, against the current of women leaving.

"I know today is the sixth anniversary," she said to me as we hugged. "Thank you for making time for me on this day."

She had read *A Temporary Gift* and remembered the date. Upon hearing those words, my usually calm and collected demeanour gave way and I crumbled.

"I should be thanking you," I said to her, crying in that embrace outside Al-Masjid Al-Nabawi. I knew she was struggling with a wound that was fresher and much more painful than mine.

As much as she felt she needed to meet me, I needed to meet her, too. I needed her to say these words into my ear, to acknowledge that the pain was still there, being worn around my neck, even though so many others couldn't see it.

The people milling about around us, looking on in curiosity, had no idea who we were or why this was an emotional embrace. We looked into each other's eyes, past our tears, and truly saw each other.

To see and be seen is a beautiful thing.

Allah (swt) had already given me one of the best gifts I had ever received by allowing me to complete my hajj. Looking at Farah standing in front of me, both of us having travelled here from places so, so far away, made me appreciate the generosity of Allah's planning. As though to show me that miracles will keep coming when you keep asking, He sent Farah to me in beautiful, peaceful Madinah.

We sat on the marble steps of the *masjid*'s entrance, knees to our chests, with the dry evening heat of Madinah enveloping us.

She told me the same thing I had thought months ago: Amr reminded her of Atta. She felt Amr's kindness come to life through *A Temporary Gift*, and her husband had many of the same traits. He was genuine, gentle, and protective.

It's a pattern I have seen and read about for years: those who are killed—and who we hope have been honoured with martyrdom—have similar qualities. They are strong, but their strength is devoid of pride and used compassionately. They are not stingy with their love and mercy. People gravitate towards them, wanting to be in the presence of the hope they radiate.

I can barely remember what we spoke about, sitting on those steps, but I remember telling her, "Allah chose you for this test and you'll be amazed at how much beauty is still yet to come in your life."

I believed it to my core.

In saying these words to her, I thought back to all the beautiful, miraculous things that have happened in my own life. And as the moon crept across the Madinah sky, the day that had started off lonely and difficult for me vanished. It was replaced with a day of immense gratitude.

I met some of the other Christchurch victims' families in Madinah that day, many of whom had come for hajj together. They had lost their brothers, spouses, and children on that fateful day.

I sat with them, listening to their voices speak and laugh, looking at their eyes, which danced so genuinely with hope and light. Although I was not surprised by their courage, I was still in awe, hoping to absorb some of it for myself.

As painful as their losses had been, Farah told me the victims' families had rallied around one another, forming a tight-knit community of support. Just a day before the massacre, these families barely knew each other, if at all. But their shared pain instantly pulled them together: a second family borne of necessity.

Sitting with them, I could have asked questions or given them words of encouragement. They, too, had read my book. But I said almost nothing. Looking into the eyes of people who were walking the same path of grief was enough. We understood, without saying much, the fire we'd all been walking through and the hurt we'd had to make space for in our hearts.

I've seen many evils in my life, but I've also seen great kindness come afterwards. I'm reminded of the verse in the Qur'an where the angels ask Allah (swt) why He would create a creature who would bring corruption to the earth and spill blood, and He replies:

{...I know that which you do not know.}

(Baqarah 2: 30)

Through my tragedy, I've been able to see so much good that I never knew was there. I've seen love, empathy, and gestures that make me hopeful for our community's future. I've met with people like beautiful Farah and shared some of the most special moments with them. And it reminds me of Allah's powerful statement:

{...I know that which you do not know.}

We submit to Him fully—to His knowledge and to His purpose for us. If we are looking, He will show us our path, and He will bring us everything we need to worship Him. The hurts, the smiles, the struggles are all there for a reason.

Truly, He knows what we don't know.

I never would have met Farah or the other families had I not walked this precise path Allah had set out for me. They never would have found comfort and healing in my writing had I not lived through the pain of losing Amr.

I am grateful, more than anything, for my Lord, Who intimately knows the condition of my heart. He continuously brings me the experiences, reminders, and people who inspire me to be courageous, who remind me of my purpose, and who lift my heart higher than I ever believed possible.

In my loneliest, darkest moments as I frantically attempt to scrape together an extra ounce of patience, I always find Allah, Most High, reassuring me that there is a meaning and purpose behind my struggle.

I always find a bright spot on the path, a meaningful hug, or a moving sentence spoken into my ear to help me keep going.

This is His mercy, and His mercy encompasses all things.

My life in orbit

When my daughter was four years old, she asked me one night in bed before drifting off, "Where does the sun go when it's nighttime?" She thought that the sun went to sleep whenever it disappeared from the sky.

"It doesn't go to sleep," I said to her. "It just goes to other places and other countries."

She was satisfied with the answer, though I knew she didn't quite understand it.

Then I started thinking, *The sun is always setting somewhere*. Always and without fail, twenty-four hours a day, it sets again and again, inching its way across the globe. It never stops setting, actually. It just depends on where you're standing.

But at night, most of us don't really think about the sun. We don't wonder where it is or what it's doing. We don't say, "Why, God, did you take the sun away?"

We don't cry for the sun when it disappears below the farthest edge of the horizon. We understand that this is how our world works: day, then night. Light, then darkness. We know that in a matter of a few hours, the sun will be back and will make everything bright and beautiful again.

Just like the alternation of night and day, our lives alternate between joy and sadness, love and heartache, blessings and deprivation.

Allah (swt) says:

{Indeed, in the creation of the heavens and the earth and the alternation of the night and the day are signs for those of understanding.} *(Al Imran 3: 190)*

We need the day to work and live, and we need the night to rest and recharge. We need joy and love to energize and motivate us, but we sometimes need heartache and deprivation to contemplate the brevity of our existence and fortify our gratitude to God.

The world in which we live, however, doesn't want us to accept that there are moments of darkness that *must* be experienced. We attempt to mute our uncomfortable, painful feelings with whatever entertainment keeps our senses buzzing. Reality is too difficult, so we seek an escape from it.

This is precisely the reason I avoided watching TV shows or movies for a full year after Amr passed away.

I didn't actually make the decision consciously, or specifically set a one-year timer on it. That's just how long it naturally lasted. When I would come upon someone in my household watching TV, I couldn't bring myself to sit with him or her. I couldn't withstand what I felt would just distract and numb me. I knew there was meaning in what had happened to me. If I was going to find it, I would have to quiet my mind and heart.

To those around me, it seemed like an unreasonable knee-jerk reaction, especially considering how much of our social interactions revolved around consuming entertainment. I wanted to feel everything, though, and numbing my pain without addressing it was counterintuitive.

Instead, I met the darkness when it came. When the grief knocked at my door and wanted to enter, I let it in. I examined it and explored its shapes and dimensions. I sought to know it intimately because I felt that without truly knowing it, I could never emerge from it.

All the while, I knew in my heart of hearts that light and joy would come knocking at my door again.

In time, my no-TV resolution was chipped away and I resumed a more balanced relationship with entertainment. I started watching my favourite Food Network shows again. My daughter and I watched *Frozen*. I started an Instagram account.

That being said, I wouldn't change anything

about the year I spent without all of this. It gave me enough mental space to look at my life with fresh eyes and a new perspective. I was able to undertake the *tadabbur*, or deep reflection, that was needed after such a traumatic event had taken place in my life.

Had I refused to face the trauma, my silenced emotions would have come roaring back at some point. Upon their return, they'd be different—transformed by time and experience—and they might have become more harmful to my mental health. Or perhaps I would have survived just fine even if I had indulged in a bit of entertainment here and there. But I didn't want to just survive. I wanted to grow and change and thrive.

Scholars have compiled many lists of the spiritual benefits of being tried in this world: it expiates our sins, it brings us closer to the remembrance of God, it softens our hearts towards others who are suffering, and it reminds us of our ultimate purpose to worship Him. However, if our fear of hardships makes us consistently numb ourselves, we'll miss out on that spiritual growth.

At the same time, everything is created with impeccable balance, and Allah (swt) does not burden us with more than we can bear. He gives us the joys of family, wealth, love, material success, and children to enrich our experiences and spark gratitude in our hearts.

Just as He grants us enough sunlight in our days

to work and enough darkness in our nights to rest, Allah gives us just enough joy and just enough pain for our hearts to rise and fall, to change, to thrive. If everything in our lives remained stagnant and unchanging, our spiritual states would suffer. It is precisely within those moments of change that we experience the opportunities to grow in faith, wisdom, and resilience.

Just as the sun is always setting somewhere, the sun is also always rising somewhere else. In moments of internal darkness, I love to remember a simple phrase that Allah (swt) says in the Qur'an:

{...Is not the morning near?} *(Hud 11: 81)*

Allah (swt) also says:

{And the sun runs [on course] toward its stopping point. That is the determination of the Exalted in Might, the Knowing. And the moon—We have determined for it phases, until it returns [appearing] like the old date stalk. It is not allowable for the sun to reach the moon, nor does the night overtake the day, but each, in an orbit, is swimming.} *(Ya Seen 36: 38-40)*

The moon has its place in the sky, swimming in its orbit around our globe. So, too, does the sun have its set course. They'll never catch up to one another because they are servants to His will. They have a precise purpose and place in existence.

Sometimes we feel unanchored, thrown into a life that can seem chaotic and haphazard. We can't see a bigger pattern. We can't see where our lives are headed. But just like the sun and moon have their ongoing symbiosis, we also have a precise path on which to walk.

In my first twenty-seven years on this planet, I imagined my life going a very specific way: university, husband, three or four kids, career, house, grandkids, retirement. It was clearly mapped out in my head. I wanted an average life, with average joys and average difficulties. I didn't want any more or any less.

Were it not that my husband suddenly left this earth, I wouldn't have written *A Temporary Gift*—a book thousands of people around the world have turned to in their own journeys towards healing. I wouldn't have started my company, Ruqaya's Bookshelf, which produces and publishes beautiful stories for Muslim kids. I wouldn't have taken my writing beyond the confines of personal journaling.

Right before I finished writing my book, *A Temporary Gift*, I had a dream that I was in a train station. Someone had robbed me of everything I owned. I was pacing through the crowd, frantically searching the faces of those waiting for their trains, but none were familiar or friendly.

The panic was rising in my chest, reaching up and tightening around my throat. Then I stopped and began rummaging through my pockets, searching for something that would help me. My fingers grasped a piece of paper and I pulled it out. It was crumpled and the writing was barely legible, but I knew what it was right away. I knew it was the cover of a book I would write.

When I looked at that page, a sense of peace overcame me in my sleep. I had no material possessions to speak of and no one to help me on this path. I had lost them all to thieves and murderers. But I still had this with me. This one, barely legible, wrinkled piece of paper. It was something they couldn't take from me—it was the hope in a renewed purpose. It was the hand to tug me forward when all I really wanted to do was curl up into a ball and hide away. It was a kind of foreshadowing that my orbit, my path, my purpose was not cut off. My new life was just starting.

People can take so many things from us: our belongings, our homes, and even the souls of people we love. They can ransack our lives and leave us with what seems like nothing. But they can't steal our hope or the opportunities that God puts in our paths. They can do damage to our bodies, but they can never erase faith from our hearts.

The Lord Who has a plan for the innumerable celestial bodies in our universe has a plan for you, too. There is a course in your life that needs to be run. You are meant to be here and you serve a purpose. Your path might not look as apparent and seamless as the movement of the sun and the moon, but rest assured you are on it now and Allah (swt) is well aware.

I walk forward with my daughter in one hand,

always fielding difficult questions from her like "Where do babies come from?" or "What does Allah look like?" With the other hand, I juggle my books, my family, my health—all heavy, and all asking for time and attention.

I am often overwhelmed. I don't always know where I am going. I don't always know how I will give all these responsibilities their due attention. But I know I am moving in the precise direction God intended for me. There is luminous comfort in being absolutely sure that He is holding me up on my path, exactly like everything else He created in the heavens and on the earth.

He will take me where I am meant to go. If I trust Him, I'll always find purpose and meaning along the way.

Can I stay a little longer?

On a Saturday night in early 2019, as I went into *sujood* during *'isha* prayer, I had sudden pains in my chest. With every breath, in or out, there was a stabbing sensation right around my heart. It caught me completely off guard. I quickly googled my symptoms right after I finished praying. I didn't find any results online that didn't end with something that meant that I was probably dying.

I tried waiting it out, doing breathing exercises, leaning back in a reclining chair, and lying down. I took some medication, but nothing helped. Any quick or sudden movement exacerbated the pain. I got dressed slowly and asked my sister to drive me to a nearby emergency room. I took in shallow breaths and sat as still as I possibly could, but my mind was racing. *What if this is my last night on earth?* I thought. *What if my deeds are about to be cut off forever?*

In the ER, the doctor ordered a myriad of tests and all the while I tried not to breathe too deeply or bend my body in a way that might potentially worsen the pain. As I was thinking about the possibility of dying any moment, I realized with overwhelming fear that I was utterly unprepared. My soul wasn't ready. There were too many loose ends left: too many negative words I would never be able to take back, too many good deeds I had delayed because I thought I had time, and too many piled-up sins about to come crashing down on me. I asked Allah (swt) to forgive me. Then I asked Him:

Can I stay a little longer?

It occurred to me that my daughter says these same words to me every time we have to leave a place she loves. She holds on to my sleeve and bounces up and down, pleading with her words and eyes, "Just ten more minutes?"

She hasn't gotten her fill of fun, of play, of friends. She hasn't gotten to do everything she planned on doing before I stood up and said, "It's time to go." Her little heart is devastated at the thought that her joy will soon end, her time of fun and frolic cut short.

In many ways, we are the same as children: never quite ready to leave.

Instead of taking advantage of the time we have on earth, knowing full well that it's coming to an end soon, we misuse it. All the while, the hours of our lives drip away like drops of water escaping a leaky tap. With each drop, a part of us disappears.

Allah (swt) swears by time in the Qur'an:

{By time, verily humankind is in loss...} *(al-'Asr 103: 1)*

Every human being is partaking in an invisible, unspoken battle against time. The grand deception of this *dunya* is that it sometimes feels so long. We count down to things. We cross days out on a calendar until the day we're waiting for—a graduation, a wedding, a vacation—finally arrives. But those days we cross out, the weeks we can't wait to be over, the minutes that seem to go on for hours—this is what makes up most of our lives. It's The Middle Stuff. We assign no importance to The Middle Stuff. We shove aside the ordinary, shrug-worthy, unremarkable moments. We think they mean nothing.

At the end of all of this, though, when we are standing before God and we are asked:

{How long did you remain on earth?}

some people will say:

{...A day or part of a day.} *(al-Mu'minoon 23: 112-113)*

When our souls are extracted from our bodies, we will wish we had a few more minutes to pray, to say kind words, or to give in charity. Minutes will be worth more than anything we ever possessed. There is no extra or irrelevant time on this earth. There is only precious time which we either use wisely or squander.

No one is immortal, and everyone ultimately succumbs to the battle against time—

{Except for those who have believed and done righteous deeds and advised each other to truth and advised each other to patience.} *(al-'Asr 103: 3)*

Those who make the concerted effort to hasten towards Allah (swt) and use their time on this earth to do good: they are the only ones who have actually succeeded.

Prophet Musa (as) has a beautiful statement in the Qur'an. When he ascends the mountain for his appointment with Allah (swt), he rushes there ahead of his people. Allah asks him:

{And what made you hasten from your people, O Musa?}

Musa replies:

{…I hastened to You, my Lord, that You may be pleased.} *(Ta Ha 20: 83-84)*

The love that Musa (as) had for his Lord is clearly illustrated in this one statement. He rushed up the mountain, leaving his travelling companions behind, because he was impatient to be in the company of His Lord.

Allah (swt) beseeches us:

{Race toward forgiveness from your Lord and a garden whose width is like the width of the heavens and earth, prepared for those who believed in Allah and His messengers. That is the bounty of Allah which He gives to whom He wills, and Allah is the Possessor of great bounty.} *(al-Hadeed 57: 21)*

We are told here to hurry up on this path to paradise. Don't keep looking back to compare how "far ahead" you are compared to others. Don't get discouraged by the scores of people racing past you. Don't get distracted every two minutes by people standing at the side of the road, calling you to slow down.

A race by its very nature is intense; your breathing becomes laboured, your legs eventually want to buckle, and your heart pounds through your chest. You push your body and mind to their limits in order to reach that finish line. This is what we are asked to do—to race, not dawdle.

We lose our focus every once in a while because it's human nature to get distracted and make mistakes. We might not hasten to perform good deeds, or to seek forgiveness, or to walk away from what is evil. We linger until a moment of shock comes upon us and we think, *If I were to die right now, I would not be ready.*

There is a striking nuance that's often overlooked in English translations of the Qur'an. Allah (swt) says:

{Indeed, it is We who will inherit the earth and whoever is on it, and to Us they will be returned.} *(Maryam 19: 40)*

The Arabic word in this *ayah*, *yurja'oon*, is translated as, "will be returned." In English, "will be returned" is in the future tense. The Arabic, *yurja'oon*, is in the present tense, however.

In reality, the translation is incomplete. Allah (swt) is saying that *we are returning*. In the present tense, as we are reading this, we are returning to Him. The return to Him is not some faraway event that will eventually come to pass. It's happening right now. We are walking on the paths that will lead us to our final moments. Our bodies are deteriorating and the invisible timer on our lives is counting down.

The same concept applies to the *ayah* in which Allah (swt) says:

{Every soul shall taste death...} *(al-Anbiya' 21: 35)*

The Arabic word translated as "shall taste" is actually in the present tense as well. So every soul *is tasting death* right now.

How truthful and fitting these words are! Nothing that has passed will ever come back. The portion of our lives that we have already experienced and lived out has died. The aches and pains, the illnesses, and the exhaustion that now come and go are just a small taste of an upcoming event that will not be just a health scare. It will be real.

There is no one on this earth who knows when the last time for anything will come. We have a finite amount of time to make amends with those we have wronged and to serve our families and the community. We have a finite amount of time with our children before they outgrow their dependence on us and venture out into the world. We have a finite amount of time before we ourselves outgrow this world and move on to the next.

Now is all we have to worship God. Now is what matters most.

I usually look away when a needle is about to pierce my skin, but when I was getting my blood tested this time, I didn't. The nurse calmly took a vial of my blood, then another, then another. When one vial filled, she would twist it shut, set it aside, and then replace it with the next.

The sight of the earthy red blood rushing into that clear vial was mesmerizing. I couldn't look away. It wasn't trickling, it was gushing. Almost too fast. The whole process was done in mere seconds.

When it was over, the nurse pressed a small cotton ball to my skin and taped it down. She took the vials of blood someplace else to be tested. As I sat in the waiting area, I couldn't quite shake the image of that ferociously pumped blood exiting my body.

I can't feel the blood racing through my veins right now. I'm oblivious to the fact that my body is constantly working, sending spurts of oxygenated blood to every little piece of flesh, to every fingertip and toe.

It's an unseen system—an intricately designed thing that is so essential to me being alive and well. Yet I can't see it or feel it. It just is.

How many more of these quiet, powerful systems exist within us and within this world that keep us alive?

We can barely appreciate the blessings that we can actually see—our homes, our vehicles, our food, our families. So of course the blessings that we can't see, touch, or hear sometimes remain completely unacknowledged.

The blood running through our veins, the air in our chests, the gravity that keeps us from floating off this planet, the seasons that come and go without our say, the exact placement of every celestial body in the sky... all are limitless blessings and hidden systems put into place by Allah (swt).

Allah says:

{And He gave you from all you asked of Him. And if you should count the favours of Allah, you could not enumerate them...} *(Ibrahim 14: 34)*

How strange that sometimes we can believe we're self-sufficient, independent beings when one microscopic blood clot can end our lives almost instantaneously. No matter how often we give thanks to our Creator, we will never truly be able to understand everything He does to keep us alive and to gift us the time we need to come back to His worship.

All praises are due to Allah, praises filling the heavens and the earth, and all that is between them.

In the end, every test at the hospital came back normal. They couldn't detect anything wrong with me or my heart. The doctor guessed it was just a strained muscle and advised me to take ibuprofen and get some rest.

But perhaps the words of desperation slipping from my tongue between the moments of laboured breathing were the purpose of that pain. Perhaps remembering all the unseen blessings we've been given, reflecting on our ultimate end, and relying only on Him is actually the purpose of all pain.

It is narrated that the Prophet Muhammad (saw) was pleased when he overheard a Bedouin making this *du'a*:

"O the One Whom eyes cannot see, Who cannot be imagined, Who is beyond description, Who is unaffected by happenings, Who cannot be overwhelmed by the vicissitudes of time, Who knows the weight of the mountains, the volume of the oceans, the number of falling raindrops, the number of leaves on the trees, and everything upon which the night darkens and upon which the day brightens. No sky can hide another from Him, no surface of the earth can hide another from Him, no ocean can hide anything within its depths from Him, and no mountain can conceal from Him anything within its rocks. *Make the last part of my life the best, make the best of my deeds the last, and make my best day the one in which I meet You.*"[4]

We ask the same of You, O Allah. May our final deeds be the best of all our deeds, and may we strive to be ready to meet You.

The eyes with which I see

When Amr died, a bolt loosened somewhere in my body. I felt like a desk in a classroom that wobbled every time I rested my elbows on it. I hated those desks in school. Pencils slid right off of their slanted surfaces, they made my writing uneven with each wobble, and they caught me off guard every time I forgetfully leaned on them.

My mind became a metaphor for that desk: not quite falling apart, but off balance and not as useful as it should be.

As a younger (perhaps somewhat naïve) woman, I was one of the most decisive people I knew. I was confident in the choices I made, even if the results didn't pan out as expected. When I set my mind to do something, I rarely second-guessed myself or even asked for others' opinions. In my mind's eye, indecisiveness was one of the worst characteristics a person could have.

When I got married, however, my life wasn't just about *me* anymore. It was about *Amr and me*.

He was kind, Amr. Of all the things he was that I might tell people about, he was kind first and foremost. It wasn't forced; it didn't require effort. On the first day we met, I noticed the way he listened to me talk, head tilted and eyes darting back and forth between my face and the ground. His eyes smiled easily and genuinely at the same time his mouth did. It was just his nature to be good.

It was easy to like Amr. He was a simple person in the best sense of the word: open, unassuming, respectful. We didn't love each other at first but we respected one another both as people and as believers. Out of that respect grew our love.

As our relationship progressed, I let go of my stubborn decisiveness, bit by bit.

Amr and I began to make decisions about our joint life together. When I had someone by my side who was growing with me and sincerely invested in my happiness and development, I loosened my fierce grip on the reins of decision making. I let my trust in Amr translate into accepting his input and advice when decisions had to be made.

I leaned on him, and he leaned on me.

After Amr was killed, my life was uprooted and I became detached from everything I knew. Along with the immense grief that invaded my world, I felt like all of our plans for the future had disappeared. I would sometimes close my eyes and try to imagine what my life would be like without him. In the darkness behind that screen, I found nothing. And that nothing was the scariest thing of all.

Making decisions became agonizingly stressful. *Is it the right time to buy a car? Should I accept an invitation to speak about my experiences at a conference? What school should I send Ruqaya to?*

I would wobble back and forth between my choices because I had a fear of impending trauma hanging over me. What if I made the wrong decision and added more stress to my already hanging-by-a-thread existence? What if I lost someone else I loved and relied on and I had to start this whole process yet again? I felt like the earth beneath me could shift at any moment and I'd be left alone and unprepared.

Something in me was loose and for a very long time I couldn't tighten it again.

In the months that followed Amr's death, I read a *hadith qudsi* in which Allah (swt) says:

"... My slave approaches Me with nothing more beloved to Me than what I have made obligatory upon him, and My slave keeps drawing nearer to Me with voluntary works until I love him. And when I love him, I am his hearing with which he hears, his sight with which he sees, his hand with which he seizes, and his foot with which he walks. If he asks me, I will surely give to him, and if he seeks refuge in Me, I will surely protect him."[5]

I desperately needed Allah (swt) to lead me because I certainly couldn't lead myself. I couldn't decide anything. My pain paralyzed me.

I began turning to Allah and saying, "O Allah, be the eyes with which I see, the ears with which I hear, the hand with which I seize, and the foot with which I walk."

I needed Him to take charge of my hearing, my speech, and my actions. I needed Him to guide me to listen to what would help me and comfort me. I needed Him to help me see the path forward. I needed Him to inspire me to perform the actions that needed to be done in order for me to gain His love.

Amr wasn't here for me to lean on anymore and I became aware of how much I couldn't trust my own judgment in moments of weakness. So I taught myself how to lean on and trust God, the Ever-Living. I knew He would never leave me.

And then, in the months and years after speaking those words to Allah, I did so much without ever consciously *deciding* to. I wrote an entire book without ever meaning to! *A Temporary Gift* started as disparate, short paragraphs I wrote just to make sense of my emotions. I would type what I was feeling into a Word document, then look at the words, rearrange them, and edit them until I could see what I'd written and say to myself: *What you are feeling is normal. What you are feeling makes sense.*

Those sentences and paragraphs grew longer and acquired more depth. They began intertwining in a meaningful way. They became chapters. The chapters became a book.

It sounds silly to say that a three-hundred-page book just materialized, but it truly felt effortless. When I reflect on how that book came together, I see the guidance of Allah (swt) so palpably. He said, "Be," and it was.

Whenever I feel lost and confused, I turn to Him, knowing that there is no one better in whom to put my complete trust.

Leaning on Allah (swt) opened up opportunities I never thought possible, and over the years I would see a significant growth in my decision-making abilities. I believe it all stemmed from the *du'a* that I had made in my grief for Allah (swt) to be *the eyes with which I see, the ears with which I hear, the hand with which I seize, and the foot with which I walk.*

I often think about this in the context of my car. In the middle of some errands one day, it started making an alarming clunking noise. It sounded just like a loose bolt being flung wildly about under the hood of my car. I plodded along, trying to ignore it, but the rattling kept getting louder and more obnoxious as I drove. A feeling of dread crept up my chest and sat squarely on my shoulders. I hated going to the mechanic. I hated waiting for the diagnosis and eventually forking over large sums of money to fix my rusty old car.

I hoped the sound would magically go away on its own, but it didn't. I needed help.

I stood in front of a cramped, dirty car shop, watching the mechanic bent over my car fiddle with its insides. I shifted my body's weight from foot to foot, wondering when he would have answers for me. Every errand and appointment was on hold until this problem was identified.

This was one of the things I never imagined doing a few short years ago when my feet were stuck deep in the thick mud of grief. Amr passed away before we owned a car, so I had never needed to care for or maintain one. I had never pulled into a gas station and pumped gas, taken a car in for an oil change, or stared into the mess of pipes and wires under a car's hood so I could pour in some windshield wiper fluid. The names of car parts and what could go wrong with them were a foreign language. I understood none of it.

But here I was, several years later, at a warehouse-like garage where my car was being fixed, ready to hear the mechanic's conclusion. This whole process, despite being frustrating, had become incredibly *regular*.

The car is the simplest example of the seismic shift from the first version of my grief to the second. After Amr died, I was thrust into a life of needing to get things done without waiting for outside help.

While standing in that car garage, I thought back to August 2013 and realized how "easy" I actually had it. When he died, Amr didn't leave behind a car that I had to sell, an apartment that I had to pay rent for, a phone contract that I couldn't cancel, or more than a few thousand dollars for which I had to figure out inheritance.

He was gone, and it hurt beyond anything I'd ever imagined. At the same time, my practical affairs were made incredibly easy. Before I even understood my newly-formed inability to make decisions, Allah (swt) had removed that burden from me.

I used to say, "Oh Allah! Nothing is easy except what You have made easy. If You wish, You can make the difficult easy."[6]

I would say it over and over. At the time, I didn't understand what that *du'a* would mean for me. But in the midst of all the chaos following Amr's passing, everything in the external, material world was like putty in my hands: malleable, easy, and completed without resistance.

Someone else took care of Amr's death certificate and funeral arrangements. Someone else bought my plane tickets back to Canada for me. Someone else drove me to and from all the errands I had to do.

Someone else put food on my plate at every meal and gave it to me. Someone else bought diapers and baby food for my daughter.

Allah (swt) gave me the space I needed to tend to my wounded heart without having to worry about anything else. That in and of itself was a beautiful mercy when I needed it the most. That was the ease that I had asked Him for so fervently.

Other things that would eventually come my way were not made "easier" in the literal sense of the word. Instead, the ease was manifested in Allah (swt) giving me the strength to adapt, to learn, and to stretch my abilities farther than I expected.

I put my trust in God, knowing that He would steer me right, and I stretched my heart and body to their limits.

I ballooned the love I had to give my daughter, attempting to fill the void left by Amr's departure. *I have to love her harder*, I thought to myself.

I cleared my throat, despite my jitters, and spoke at podiums to large crowds of people.

I arranged pieces of my grief like hors d'oeuvres on a platter and presented it to my followers on social media, oblivious to the reservations I probably should have had.

Everything was new and my experiences were expanding very, very quickly.

When you stretch a piece of bubble gum, you can get it to be really long—an adult's entire arm-span if it's good quality gum. But in the process of stretching it, the gum becomes thin and snaps easily. Stretch it just a millimeter too far and that's exactly what it does: snap.

Widowhood meant I had to abruptly accommodate more responsibility, love, and accountability. When I expanded my heart so suddenly, it also stretched me thin, exactly like that piece of gum. At different points in my journey, I didn't know how much farther I could stretch before something inside me snapped.

Allah (swt) tells us we're ready for every test that comes our way because:

{On no soul does Allah place a burden greater than it can bear…} *(al-Baqarah 2: 286)*

But being ready for something doesn't mean that the process of growing won't hurt. It will likely hurt a lot. You'll doubt yourself, you'll wonder if you'll ever be able to do this, and sometimes the growing pains will seem unbearable. At times, you'll snap just like that stretched piece of gum. Your patience might break, you might become angry at the world, and you might ask: *Why me?*

The beautiful ending of this story, though, is that even when a piece of gum snaps in two, it can be put back together pretty easily.

One day you wake up and realize the big, difficult things that used to stretch you to your limit have now become utterly routine. It isn't because those things have suddenly become objectively easier. It's because Allah (swt) has guided you to grow and adapt.

When you asked Allah (swt) for ease, He gave you both ease *and* growth such that you were able to victoriously stand over the difficulties that challenged you. In asking Allah (swt) to be the eyes with which you see, the ears with which you hear, the hand with which you seize, and the foot with which you walk, you gained His help in everything you did. He gave you the ability to stretch so far beyond where you believed your abilities ended.

When the mechanic finally turned around to tell me what was wrong with my car, I listened attentively. I quietly nodded as he named all the failing parts and put an astronomically high price tag on the cost of fixing and replacing them. "It's not worth it," he said. Even by his own calculations, it wasn't worth investing such a large sum into an old car that I'd likely have to replace soon anyway.

I had to make a choice. I had to decide whether to abandon this car and get a new one or to sink more money into it. To my surprise, I didn't wobble back and forth between my options. I knew what I had to do. I said *bismillah* and almost immediately started looking for a new car. In just a couple of days, I had bought one.

Now when I open the hood of my car I'm always surprised at how, with Allah's help and guidance, what was difficult yesterday has become easy today.

Allah (swt) says:

{For verily, with every hardship there is ease. Verily, with hardship there is ease.} *(al-Inshirah 94: 5-6)*

In these verses, He doesn't say, "*after* hardship there is ease." He says *with*, and He repeats it. So search for the ease that Allah has given you in the midst of your hardship and thank Him for it.

If you haven't yet seen the ease in your hardship, you may have to hold on a bit longer until it becomes clear. But know for certain that it will come because Allah (swt) never breaks His promise.

Expand for me
my chest

I stood trembling on a stage in front of a thousand listeners, my hands gripping the sides of the podium. I stared into the blindingly bright lights that shone in my eyes. I was quiet for a brief moment, scanning the audience of unfamiliar faces waiting for me to say something. I took a deep breath, knowing this exact spot where I now stood had been in Allah's plan for me far before I came into this world. I cleared my throat and began with these words in my heart and on my lips:

{My Lord, expand for me my chest, and make easy for me my task, and untie the knot from my tongue that they may understand my speech.} *(Ta-Ha 20: 25-28)*

A few weeks earlier, I had received an invitation to speak at two back-to-back Islamic conferences. First, I would speak to a crowd of one thousand listeners in New Jersey, then travel to Chicago and give that same speech to another thousand the next day.

When they first asked me to attend these events, the organizers requested that I tell my story of pain and healing. For a week after I received the invite, I kept asking myself the same question: *What makes me qualified to share a podium with the same teachers and speakers I had been learning from for years?* The intense chasm between my meager qualifications and their years of study and service was incredibly clear to me.

I hesitated, but I eventually agreed. Despite my many doubts, I couldn't reject the opportunity to tell my husband's story.

An hour before my first speech in New Jersey, I was in my hotel room preparing. My skirt, shirt, and hijab were laid out on the bed, freshly ironed. I had practiced my speech many times on the flight there and again in my room. I placed my notes on the ironing board (pretending it was the podium), looked at myself in the mirror, and gestured appropriately. Every word came out exactly as I had intended.

Still, I felt unsure of myself. I was out of my league, an imposter. No matter what words I used or how appropriately I gestured, surely everyone in that crowd would see right through me.

I paced back and forth, the thick hotel carpet muting the sound of my footsteps. The eerie quiet of my room contrasted with the warring voices in my head.

The voices were questioning me aggressively, accusing me of taking opportunities I didn't deserve. *What could you say that would come even close to the powerful and informed speeches being given by the other speakers and scholars on that stage? What if you embarrass yourself? Did you consider your intentions properly before coming?*

The questions swirled in my mind, causing a cluttered, queasy mess in my gut.

As though to shield myself from these doubts, I repeated Musa's *du'a*: *My Lord, expand for me my chest, and make easy for me my task, and untie the knot from my tongue that they may understand my speech.*

To distract myself, I flipped open my laptop and logged on to Facebook. I noticed a message notification pop up. There was a message waiting for me from a woman who had read my book, *A Temporary Gift*. I had received many messages before, but this one was different.

She had been married to a Muslim man for many years but could not bring herself to embrace her husband's faith. Islam was still foreign to her and she was holding it at a distance. She said that Allah (swt) was never a "personal" God to her—

she couldn't connect with Him emotionally in a way that was meaningful. My book changed that for her. She was able to see, through the lens of my grief and through my struggle to maintain hope and patience, that Allah (swt) is very much a part our lives. My writing showed her that He was present with us in an intimate, beautiful, and awe-inspiring way.

She had decided to embrace Islam.

I read the message again, line by line, not sure if I had read it correctly the first time. Then I leaned back in my chair and let a hot mess of tears roll down my face.

Through the message, I found clarity. I was here for a reason. I was in this hotel room, about to get dressed and walk into a roomful of a thousand people for a reason. If the words I had written from inside my own darkness were enough to reach across vast spaces and change someone's heart, then surely there was a reason for them.

Sometimes I don't know all the reasons. Sometimes in darker moments I wish I understood the "whys" better than I do. Sometimes I doubt the things I say or do can touch anyone's heart or change anyone's life for the better.

Then Allah sends me a message as though to say: *There is a reason for you. There has always been a reason for you.*

Allah (swt) sends us moments of clarity to free us from the clutches of debilitating doubt, to quiet the whispers that infiltrate our hearts saying, *There are a million better people than me and I'm not qualified to be doing anything.*

Even if people make you feel worthless and without talent, merit, or purpose, there's a reason for you. Even if you're lost and you feel like you can't move forward, there's a reason for you. Even with all your faults, your mistakes, and your doubts, there's a reason for you.

Even if you can't see it at this moment, Allah does. That's why you're here. So bloom ferociously and without fear of being crowded out or trampled upon. Your Lord is the Most Generous. He has measured out for you your sustenance of sun and water and air, no matter what clouds seem to loom above.

He brought you forward as a seed in your mother's womb. Even before that, He knew you as just a written word in a record that is kept high above. He placed you in this very spot, on this plot of land, before there was even anything to be placed, before the heavens and earth exploded into existence.

He decided you mattered enough to be here. He said, "Be," and you were.

You. Exactly you.

I put my clothes on, walked straight towards that conference room full of strangers, and spoke into that microphone. My stomach was knotted up, but my words rang clear and loud. I didn't stutter because of Prophet Musa's beautiful *du'a* that I had been repeating for days. I said my husband's name during my speech, and that meant something to me. I was hugged, I was welcomed into people's hearts, and I was satisfied that Allah had brought me here.

After my speech, I sat at a table to sign copies of my book. The lineup to purchase my book was long; in the span of a few minutes, the books were sold out.

As I was getting ready to leave, an elderly man and his granddaughter came to speak to me. They explained with great sadness in their eyes that they were at the same peaceful march as my husband in Alexandria on August 16, 2013. They made *du'a* for Amr and left me with words of reassurance and comfort.

Since I started writing about my husband, I've met with survivors of the Rabaa massacre, with widows, and with many other people wrestling with grief. They seek me out. Each time I speak with them, their eyes search mine, desperate to claw at some semblance of relief from their distress.

I used to wonder what all those searching eyes had in common. Why did they all look at me the same way? What exactly were they searching for?

Our conversations were mostly very short, made up of pleasantries and some exchanged *du'as*. None of them asked to sit and chat over a meal or talk to me at length. But there was always a need in their hearts as they approached me.

They needed to look into the eyes of a person who had felt the same kind of heartache: someone who had journeyed through the same thorny path that they were currently traversing *and survived*. When they embraced me, I felt them release the heaviness they were holding in their arms and chests. I saw the tears they had been holding back stream down their faces.

We connect with people who have gone through similar struggles. We see something in them—some light, some hope, some flicker of patience that we want for ourselves. We gravitate towards one another, pulled close by an invisible but powerful connection.

This is one of the reasons there is such beauty and truth in the life of our Messenger (saw). When I read about the grief he felt after losing his beloved wife, his children, and his Companions, I feel the grief as though it were my own. My heart is drawn to his life. When I hear about the ways his family and Companions suffered at the hands of oppressors, I know he felt the same (and more) sorrow I feel when I watch my loved ones living under oppression. In learning how he was forced to escape his home in fear, seeking refuge for himself and his family in a foreign place, I know that my feelings of strangeness are not strange at all. He felt them, too.

We were created as social beings, always searching for someone with whom to connect over shared experiences. There is no test that we go through except that the Prophet (saw) went through the same or worse. Studying his *seerah*, I see the utter, sometimes painful, humanity of his life. I gravitate towards his example because of a deep-rooted connection I feel to him.

Ironically, in response to the prophethood of Muhammad (saw), the disbelievers would say:

{What is this messenger that eats food and walks in the markets? Why was there not sent down to him an angel so he would be with him a warner?} *(al-Furqan 25: 7)*

Little did they realize that it was exactly *because* of his real and tangible humanity that generations of people have been able to relate to his message and life.

In a beautiful *hadith* about the importance of human connection and brotherhood, Prophet Muhammad (saw) said:

"The most beloved of people according to Allah is he who brings the most benefit, and the most beloved of deeds according to Allah—the Mighty, the Magnificent—is that you bring happiness to a fellow Muslim, relieve him of distress, pay off his debt, or stave away hunger from him. It is more beloved to me that I walk with my Muslim brother in his time of need than that I stay secluded in the mosque for a month."[7]

The moment we remove our vulnerability, humanity, and personal connection from our faith, the farther we stray from the beauty of Prophet Muhammad's example. Islam is meant to be practiced by human beings who are flawed and in pain, who struggle to succeed but sometimes fail, and who return to God after those failures. It is not meant to be practiced by flawless beings who feel nothing and struggle with nothing.

Prophet Muhammad (saw) said:

"By Him in Whose hand is my soul, if you did not sin, Allah would replace you with people who would sin and they would seek forgiveness from Allah and He would forgive them."[8]

Our most basic and raw sense of humanity is intrinsically woven into the very fabric of our relationship with Allah (swt).

Reading that woman's Facebook message and subsequently walking up to that podium, I began to understand that people connect with my story because they see and understand my humanity. From the very first moments after losing Amr, I said clearly: *I am not ashamed to expose my struggles or fears. I do not hold back from publicly reflecting on my grief.*

I treasure the moments Allah (swt) allows me to give voice to something that is not often spoken about or something that has slipped the collective memory of our communities. I know it brings a wave of comfort to the hearts of people who have been suffering in silence. It brings to light the fact that our humanity is what connects us to each other, to our pious predecessors, and to Allah (swt).

If I had rejected the offer to speak at the conferences and all the subsequent talks I've given, these words would never have travelled from my heart to the hearts of those I spoke to. They would have remained unsaid, imprisoned someplace in my chest. But those words were meant to be released and my chest was meant to be widened through that process.

And in turn, I was meant to be held by grieving arms so that I, too, could be assured that I was not alone. I was meant to be spoken to softly by those who have walked in my shoes and to be comforted by people whose hearts have opened and blossomed despite witnessing so much injustice. When we are able to connect with one another through our words, we are lifted from emotional and spiritual seclusion.

Any time I feel there are words and emotions stuck in my chest, I repeat the *du'a* of Musa with the expectation that Allah (swt) will help me release them, smoothing my tongue so I may express them in a beautiful way. And without fail, He does just that. *Alhamdu lillah*.

A home near You

The days that followed my husband's death have become a foggy mess in my mind; partly because of the years that have passed and partly because I have consciously pushed them into a dark corner of my memory. There are, however, some memories that have followed me closely—memories of insensitivity and betrayal that have left jagged scars across the surface of my heart.

When we confirmed the news that Amr had indeed been shot and killed, my mother-in-law—almost immediately and instinctively—rearranged her living room. She found all the chairs in the apartment and set them up in a sort of semicircle next to the couches in the sitting area. Any piece of furniture that wasn't essential and couldn't be sat on was pushed up against the wall to make space for visitors.

We had visitors right away on Friday, the same day Amr was shot, and the rest trickled in over the course of the next week. They didn't call in advance or let us know when they'd be dropping by. They just came. I was mostly grateful for them: for their distracting faces and voices, for the respite they gave me by holding my daughter in their arms for a few moments so I could splash water on my face and try to understand who the person was who was looking back at me in the washroom mirror.

Some visitors, though, came begrudgingly out of social decorum, out of politeness, or out of a desire to seem empathetic to the widow and the orphan. These were the ones who sighed and rolled their eyes and *tried* (but failed) to hold their tongues.

Amr's death was controversial in the eyes of some Egyptians. They blamed him for being a conscientious objector to the atrocities that were happening across the country.

Those who marched or demonstrated anti-coup sentiment were smeared by the media's propaganda machine as "traitors" and "terrorists." They were "deserving" of whatever happened to them. Media channels even refused to air reports of the August 14 massacre of over a thousand protesters in Rabaa Square.[9] Those who did cover the massacre were severely inaccurate in their reporting, going so far as to blame the deaths on the protesters themselves. I heard an Egyptian taxi driver being interviewed on the news and he nonchalantly said that they shouldn't have been there, blocking Cairo traffic—and they were terrible people anyway.

Amr marched peacefully on Friday, August 16, along with thousands of other Egyptians, so that he could be counted amongst those who objected to the unrestrained, catastrophic spilling of innocent blood. For that act, he was vilified by some of the very people who should have been in my corner.

The betrayal came right along with the hugs after Amr died. I stood at the centre of the living room with people milling about around me, as though I were in a time-lapse sequence. They came to hug me, one by one. People I knew. People I didn't know.

One of the visitors had the nerve to cry as she held me, wetting the neck of my brown and white striped hijab. She wanted to be comforted, so I did what I thought was the right thing. I patted her on her back and said, *It's going to be okay.* Then she picked up her shiny black faux leather purse with a fat gold buckle on it and left. That same woman would later log on to Facebook to announce her utter hatred of the protestors.

People came and went. I didn't even know their names. I let them see me, as though I were an animal crying behind steel bars at the dusty Alexandria zoo. I let them hug me, even though some of them had hatred tucked inside of them. I thought their tears and sad eyes would protect me from their tongues, but I was wrong.

After Amr's death, a member of my extended family casually said to my brother, "The only way to stop these protests from now on is to find out who the protesters are, go to their homes, and kill their families."

My brother did not know how to respond, so he didn't.

In the very living room where people came to "comfort" Amr's family, yelling matches broke out between those who thought the killings were wrong and those who maintained that the killings were justified.

At the time I said nothing. I was frozen in grief, exhausted, unable to vocalize the *How dare you?* that was clinging to the tip of my tongue.

These are words that I have lived with, that have pressed themselves upon me, branding my skin with marks of betrayal. As much as I have tried to forget, the words come back every time these members of my family are mentioned in my home.

From almost the moment I experienced this until today, I have repeated the *du'a* of Aasiya (as), the wife of the Pharaoh, as she was being tortured by Pharaoh's men:

{My Lord, build for me, near You, a home in paradise.} *(at-Tahreem 66: 11)*

Aasiya was tortured to death by the order of her own husband because she believed in the message of guidance that Musa (as) brought to his people. The person who was supposed to be in her corner betrayed her. Pharaoh was someone who, by the very nature of his relationship to her, should have shown some mercy or at least some kind of restraint.

I also thought the people closest to me would hold me up and be my staunchest supporters. They were, after all, my blood. I thought they might at least hold their tongues from saying hurtful things about Amr. I thought they'd see me in my grief-induced detachment and disbelief and have enough mercy to withhold their vitriol until I was out of earshot.

Unfortunately, it didn't always happen that way.

I can't imagine being in the position of Aasiya, knowing that because of her husband's cruelty her death was imminent. In the moment before her death, Aasiya could have recanted her faith, begged for her life, or offered her torturers riches and wealth if they allowed her to escape. Instead, she shed her attachment to this world, turned her face towards the sky, and asked her Lord to give her a home in paradise. But before she asked for the home, she specified the location of that home in her *du'a*:

{Build for me, *near You*, a home in paradise.}

Nearness to her Creator was her priority. The actual home came second.

Using her *du'a* taught me that I also had the ability to tear myself away from the betrayal that I had experienced and from the torture that was inflicted upon my heart. It taught me not to dwell on anything except what really mattered: being in the honoured company of my Creator in the afterlife.

I have learned that when I open myself up to people, when I lower my guard for a moment and decide to be vulnerable, or when I gather the courage to say what I feel, I will inevitably get hurt.

Someone will betray my secrets. Someone will laugh at my vulnerabilities. Someone will light my heart on fire—like some of those women in that living room who came to "comfort" me. Sometimes they will do it on purpose, sometimes out of ignorance.

My relationship with the Creator is different, though. I can pour out every secret to Him and know that I will never be betrayed. I can easily whisper my fears and dreams up towards the sky. I can raise my hands and say, "I am so sad" or "furious" or "disappointed"—all while knowing that He loves to hear from His servants.

Nothing but love, mercy, and forgiveness come from opening up to the Most Merciful. We know He is shy to leave empty hands that are raised in supplication.[10]

Still, we persist in seeking comfort, sustenance, and love elsewhere. Then we become surprised when we are met with ridicule or hurt.

There are many wonderful souls wandering this earth, opening their hearts to people like you and me. Yet even with them, even in their warmest embraces and kindest words, you will not find the depth of comfort that palms open towards the sky and a heart open towards Allah (swt) can give you.

I have learned not to argue with people who hold negative views about my husband's death. If I did, every cell within me would be constantly lit with a ferocious anger.

Instead, I choose detachment from their words and beliefs. I choose to prioritize things that bring me fulfillment and joy. I choose to incorporate Aasiya's *du'a* into my life to remind myself that every pain I feel will be removed when I am in the company of my Lord, *in sha' Allah*.

Years later, I taught my daughter this *du'a*. Every night before she sleeps, she has a list of *du'as* that she recites in her small, sleepy voice. One of them is: "My Lord, build for us, near You, a home in paradise."

May we live with the conviction that meeting Allah (swt) will melt away every pain and every betrayal we have faced in this life.

Conversations
with God

When Ruqaya was a few months old, she was barely sleeping for an hour at a time. I would lay her on the bed next to me and sing to her Dawud Wharnsby's *nasheed*, "Lullaby."

In your name, Oh Lord, I lay to sleep
to rise in the morning, by your leave.
If you take my soul from me as I rest
please forgive me.
And if I wake in the morning again to a new and bright day,
then I pray you will always guide me
upon the straight way.[11]

On our visit to Egypt, whenever it was time for Ruqaya's nap, I sang it softly into her ear. I made sure everyone was quiet. I closed the shutters outside the windows, then pulled the curtains over them to minimize the intense Egyptian sunlight streaming in. But the room would never get totally dark. It was bathed in yellow streaks of sun sneaking in through the shutter's slanted openings.

I sang with some hope, rubbing my own eyes—weary and sore from jetlag—looking at my baby struggle against sleep as though it were an abhorrent thing.

When I got the news that Amr had been shot and killed, I didn't have a moment—not one single moment—to burst into tears, curl up on our bed, or stare blankly at that sun-lined wall in our room without Ruqaya seeing me.

So I held it in. I pulled in the corners of my grief like a drawstring bag, trapping it in my chest. Only God knows how much I held in so Ruqaya wouldn't see her mother openly in distress. My grief didn't allow me to put my mothering on hold. It didn't allow me to retreat from my responsibilities of making sure she was fed and changed and rested and loved.

The lullaby I sang to her didn't change. I sung it softly into her ear on the very same day I got the news. She still had to nap, even as my mind searched for relief in every dark corner it could find. We still had to go out to buy her diapers. I still had to cook and mash up food for her. She was still the priority, though I felt as if my body would at any moment

Conversations with God

become paralyzed with shock and fear.

I sang her to sleep in that room, commanding my voice not to waver, not to quiver, not to violently tear open and let out the screams it was holding in. I ordered it, and it mostly obeyed.

To this day, if I hear that *nasheed* or if I find myself absentmindedly singing its words, I am immediately transported back to that room—the room with sharp streaks of sunlight marking the walls. The room that refused to be dark, even as the darkness of my grief consumed me. I am taken there as though it is August 16, 2013 and my grief is brand new again, breathing pain into my limbs and heart.

As time passed, different sounds and sights and smells would ignite that fiery pain again: the sound of gunshots on a TV show, the sight of a shrouded body at a *janazah*, or even the scent of Amr's perfume on another man passing by me in a grocery store.

I find myself reliving my pain again and again, triggered by things that are seemingly commonplace. I find myself strangely afraid of being abandoned by the other people in my life. I find myself isolated, inhabiting a grief cocoon of my own making.

The concept of triggers wasn't foreign to me because I had completed my Masters of Social Work a few years prior. I knew about it all in theory, but until I experienced it myself, I didn't actually *get it*. I didn't realize that being triggered was going to be an ongoing psychosomatic experience.

At first, I didn't know what was happening to me. Why was I feeling so wound up and on edge? Why was I experiencing bouts of anxiety and inexplicable anger? Why was I getting recurring headaches and back pain when the doctor told me I was perfectly healthy?

I thought that as long as I didn't feel *really sad*, I was fine.

Sometimes I knowingly push away my emotional and physical reactions to my triggers, unable or unwilling to deal with them. I swallow some painkiller and distract myself with replying to e-mails so I don't have to entertain the pain. I fear that should I face my triggers head on, I will become debilitated by their intensity.

Ironically, avoiding them only allows them to build up—sometimes little pebbles one at a time, sometimes heavy bricks laid one on top of the other in compact rows around my heart. When enough of them have built up, I find myself angry, irritable, or upset for a prolonged period of time. I easily snap at my daughter, I stop responding to my friends' messages, and I stay away from writing anything meaningful.

I've let the pain gather and pool in my chest without a drain or any opening for even a single drop to escape. By refusing to acknowledge the power of my triggers, I allow them to have free, unfiltered access to my mind.

Whenever this happens, I ask myself, *When was the last time I actually examined and admitted my frustration, my ongoing grief, and my pain to Allah (swt)?* I try to recall the last time I really had a conversation with Allah.

Usually I find that it has been a while (maybe a long, long while) since I have made the kind of *du'a* that comes from a place of genuine need.

The *du'a* doesn't have to be long or articulate. It doesn't have to be well thought out. I don't have to be sitting on my prayer mat in the quiet of night with my palms facing the sky. I don't have to begin or end with the usual formalities (though they are really important sometimes). My calling out to Him doesn't have to be any of those things, and maybe it *shouldn't* always be. Because when I delay my *du'a* in order to find a "better" moment of concentration, that moment rarely comes.

Many of us were brought up with a strict definition of what a *du'a* should look and sound like. We're taught *du'as* the same way we're taught science and math: strictly formulaic and with very little wiggle room.

While there are important etiquettes of *du'a* that should be upheld and valued as often and as much as possible, heartfelt *du'as* must be paired with them. I don't believe in simply reciting *du'as* that have no meaning or effect on my heart. Instead, I believe that whatever situation I find myself in can be used to fuel the strength of my relationship and conversations with Allah (swt).

The *du'as* that have yielded the most relief for me have always been the ones I blurted out without thinking first, without adding filters or wondering, *Should I really be saying this to Allah?* They come with no preconceived notions of piety, no routinely uttered phrases. I just say exactly what I need to say. I give my words permission to spill out as they need to and to flow directly from my heart.

I remember one such instance very well. It came after weeks of bottling up my emotions to the point where I felt as though I were paralyzed. I was irritated at everyone and everything. I was prickly to the touch and unable to pinpoint why I was so angry. After dropping my daughter at school one day, instead of driving off as usual, I proceeded to the parking lot and turned off the car. I opened my window, looked up at the sky and said, "O Allah, I'm so angry. I'm just so angry and I don't know how to fix it." That's all I said, again and again, crying until there weren't any more tears in me to cry.

I've called upon Allah (swt) many times, in many situations, but this time was different. I didn't hold back. I didn't think, *Hey, is this a polite thing to say to God?*

And because I didn't hold back, I immediately felt relieved. The process of transforming emotions into words, then transferring those words from my heart to my lips and saying them to Allah, was incredibly healing. Whatever was caged inside my chest at that moment was freed.

It reminded me of Maryam's mother, when she said to Allah, in a state of shock and disbelief:

{...My Lord, I have delivered a female...} *(Al Imran 3: 36)*

She had dedicated the child in her womb to the service of Allah (swt), assuming that it would be a boy. Of course, Allah already knew what she would deliver and that this child would grow up to be the best woman of all time.

I marvel at her "*du'a*" because it begins so earnestly, so honestly. She's telling Allah (swt) something that He obviously already knows very well! As readers of this statement, we might think, *Why would she say something to God that He already knows?* But she still vocalizes it, expressing herself so easily to Him. This shows the depth of her relationship with Allah (swt)—a bond that was cultivated through remembering Him and calling out to Him in all moments.

When I say to Allah, "I'm so angry and I don't know how to fix it," He already knows that, too. He already knows everything. The point isn't to tell Him something He doesn't know. That's impossible. The point is for me to surrender myself by using whatever emotional state I'm in to gain closeness to Him. A part of that is expressing what I'm genuinely feeling and expecting true relief to come while I stand at His door.

There is no *du'a*, no calling out to Him, and

no seeking His help that is left without reply. The Prophet (saw) said:

"Verily your Lord is Generous and Shy. If His servant raises his hands to Him (in supplication) He becomes shy to return them empty."[12]

Allahu akbar! You will always leave with something beautiful and good when you call out to Him.

I often remember the statement of Ya'qoub as he was grieving his missing son:

{...I only complain of my suffering and my grief to Allah...} *(Yusuf 12: 86).*

He was not ashamed to own his grief. His pain wasn't suppressed in order to hold up some false image of "patience." He didn't pretend that he had moved on from his love of Yusuf. He said to Allah exactly what He was feeling. In return, Prophet Ya'qoub is described as having *beautiful* patience.

Bottling it up and ignoring my triggers can actually wreak havoc on me. It fuels my anger, it isolates me from those I love, and it builds the potential for serious mental illnesses to take hold.

Having faith and trust in Allah does not mean shutting down our humanity or denying the things that bring us pain. Rather, it's about owning everything that makes us human and turning to God, even with all our deficiencies. We turn to Him knowing that we are in perpetual need and He is the only One Who can respond to that need. Opening up a line of conversation with Allah (swt) where you don't hold back is the beginning of healing.

{Say, "Whether you conceal what is in your chests or reveal it, Allah knows it. And He knows that which is in the heavens and that which is on the earth. And Allah is over all things competent."} *(Al Imran 3: 29)*

Allah (swt) is *al-Fattah*, the Opener. Sometimes that means He opens a pocket in my grief so it may flow out and not drown me. Or perhaps He opens a window so that I can experience the light of day instead of getting too comfortable in the dark recesses of my own mind. Or He opens an opportunity for relief and mercy that I don't deserve, but that He gives freely anyway.

Many years later, "Lullaby" still takes me back to the day Amr was killed. Perhaps it always will. But I have learned to name and confront it. I don't let this or any other trigger hide in my chest until it becomes unbearably painful. Instead, I immediately follow it with words of remembrance.

I have learned to call out to Him in every circumstance, in every place, in every emotional state.

I have learned that *du'a*, at its essence, is not some formal meeting bound by strict procedures and exact wording.

It is a lifeline to keep my heart alive.

It is a rope to grasp when I'm drowning.

It is a place of refuge when the entire world feels like a den of lost dreams.

Replace envy
with awe

There is no easy way to say this, but: I am a social media influencer. A small fry influencer, but an influencer nonetheless.

I discovered this in the spring of 2019 while sitting in a small auditorium, about to be introduced as a speaker. The emcee rattled off a few facts about me, then ended with, "Asmaa is also a social media influencer."

What?

It gave me pause because I've read the research. I know how much damage can be caused by a culture that insists on putting overly filtered influencers on pedestals and presenting their lives as #goals to which the rest of us should aspire. Researchers are finding that the younger generation is feeling more socially isolated than ever before. Their social media interactions lead them to have more depression, anxiety, and body image insecurities.[13]

It hadn't occurred to me that I would ever genuinely be called an *influencer*. I didn't connect with the label, even though by all accounts it did apply to me.

I wanted no part in it because of my own warped experience as a social media user. I'm fed carefully constructed lies of perfection every time I scroll through my Instagram or Facebook feeds.

Everyone on my feed has a perfectly contoured nose and perfectly clear skin. Everyone has an amazing, coordinated outfit for every occasion. Everyone is well read and has these adorable, perfectly behaved kids that are a constant joy to be around. Everyone eats healthy, organic food and goes to the gym daily. Everyone takes perfect, picturesque vacations.

Apparently, anyway.

When on the receiving end of all this heavily filtered, seemingly "perfect" content and all these flawless images, who wouldn't start to believe (even subconsciously) that perfect lives exist?

And if perfect lives exist, why don't I have one? Why am I the only one struggling with loads of laundry and a kid who makes life messy and complicated? Why am I struggling to find something to wear that isn't wrinkled or stained with my child's grimy handprints? Why am I struggling to find time to read a good book or care about my eating and health habits? Why am I struggling with my emotional and mental wellbeing?

Social media platforms actively encourage their users to show their lives in the most flawless, perfect ways possible. It's built right into their very algorithms, so it's unfair to blame individual influencers for this phenomenon. A simple Google search will reveal tons of articles on *how to get more social media followers* that emphasize posting phenomenal, unblemished, bright photos and videos. They stress the importance of posting daily and not daring to take a break. In failing to follow this advice, your content garners less engagement from followers and the platform will automatically show less of your content to your followers.

In my own social media usage, I can attest to the truth of this. Social media asks me to post the most beautiful parts of my life. Constantly. The pressure to portray perfection and inspiration to my followers often has me believing that these are the only parts of me that are valid. While I want people to be able to engage and connect with my posts and writing, I also don't want to be dishonest about my life. The dishonesty feeds right back into the system that makes us believe perfect lives exist.

Before I understood the ramifications of my social media usage, I threw myself into it. It was a way to connect with other people experiencing the same grief. It was a platform to write about Amr and send it out into the world. But my interactions were setting me up as a motivational/inspirational writer and influencer. Once that persona was established, there wasn't space for me to express much else.

What my readers don't know about me is that I struggle far more than I let on. While I post inspirational quotes and happy photos, I also grapple with my emotional and spiritual health, with strained family relationships, and with a list of bad habits.

In other words, I'm human.

The dichotomy between my real life and my social media persona becomes even more apparent whenever I meet my readers in person. I've bumped into my readers while shoe shopping with my daughter and while eating dinner at a restaurant with my family. It even happened during hajj, in a hotel near the *Haram*.

I love speaking with people who appreciate my work. It tells me that when I express myself with authenticity, my words have a positive effect. Still, each time I find a reader standing in front of me, it catches me off guard. They often come towards me with open arms and unassuming eyes, ready to be inspired by words of faith and wisdom. I try to piece together a few meaningful words for them, and I'm sometimes left feeling like two different people: the flawed person I actually am and the "inspirational writer" I show the world. While I do my best not to portray my life and work as perfect, the medium allows me to go only so far.

As both a social media creator and consumer, I acknowledge that one of the greatest tests of using this medium is keeping my feelings of ingratitude at bay. When I choose to consistently expose my eyes and heart to people who seem to have more or better things, ingratitude becomes a parasite that attaches itself to my faith and slowly drains its life force. No blessing will ever seem good enough for an ungrateful heart.

One summer, I watched an influx of Instagram stories posted by some social media moms. Almost every day they would post beautiful photos and videos of their kids out and about on scenic hikes, at great restaurants around the city, and at zoos and museums.

The posts were objectively lovely, but I didn't like what they sparked in my heart. Looking at the dynamic life they led, it felt like I wasn't doing enough for my daughter. I certainly wasn't always going on hikes like that, or eating at restaurants that often, or going to awesome museums and learning centres. While they were doing all of those cool activities with their kids, my daughter and I were probably sitting on our couch eating microwaved hot dogs and watching *Kids Baking Championship* on the Food Network.

Logically, I knew full well I was doing the absolute best I could for Ruqaya, having stretched my abilities to their limit. I also knew that these women probably had lives just as messy as mine, but they (like most) chose to share only the most beautiful parts. Still, my feelings of inadequacy didn't go away.

Instead of feeling ungrateful for my own life and capabilities, I decided to try something new. I simply clicked the "mute" button and just like that, those feelings went away. It was a transformative experience for me.

I have learned that in order to protect my gratitude and emotional wellness, I have to adopt a selfish framework of self-preservation when it comes to social media. I will be perfectly candid: I have unfollowed countless influencers who constantly post lovey-dovey photos of their spouses, fabulous shots of their travel adventures, or fashion tutorials I know I can never live up to.

As a widow, watching love blossom between couples is alienating and lonely. As someone without endless disposable income to travel the world, watching people explore new places sometimes makes me feel sheltered and uncultured. As someone who genuinely doesn't have the energy to put together beautiful outfits, looking at flawlessly styled women just exacerbates my feelings of inadequacy. Social media creators are not at fault for posting these things, but the way in which I *personally* interacted with these posts had become problematic for me. They caused me to feel twinges of ingratitude and resentment towards my own life.

Not everyone is the same, though. Each one of us approaches the world with a unique set of experiences, traumas, and biases. Consequently, each one of us interacts with images, words, and content in a different way. Because of how unique our experiences are, we have to be able to mentally check in with ourselves and evaluate how what we are consuming affects us.

I knew certain content was negatively affecting me, so I had to stop consuming it.

Some may believe that this practice of self-preservation is lazy and that the better option would be to practice gratitude *despite* what I see. However, consider the statement of Prophet Muhammad (saw), who said:

"Look at those who are beneath you and do not look at those who are above you, for it is more suitable that you should not consider as less the blessing of Allah."[14]

Gratitude is a choice we make every day. Part of that is choosing not to overindulge in the minute details of others' lives. Instead, we should focus on the beautiful things we have and how best to use them to serve others.

At the same time, it isn't always possible to look past what others possess, nor should we isolate ourselves from the lives of those close to us under the guise of not wanting to become engrossed in their blessings. However, the way in which we respond to seeing others' blessings is important in determining our relationship with Allah (swt).

Prophet Zakariyah (as) was entrusted with the guardianship of Maryam (as) while she was secluded in her worship and dedication to Allah (swt) at Bayt ul-Maqdis. When he came to check on her, he found that she had fruits that were not in season. His reaction to this is recorded in this beautiful series of verses:

{Every time Zakariyah entered upon her in the prayer chamber, he found with her provision. He said, "O Maryam, from where is this [coming] to you?" She said, "It is from Allah. Indeed, Allah provides for whom He wills without account." At that, Zakariyah called upon his Lord, saying, "My Lord, grant me from Yourself a good offspring. Indeed, You are the Hearer of supplication."} *(Al Imran 3: 37-38)*

When Prophet Zakariyah saw that Maryam had provisions that seemed to appear out of thin air and fruits that were not even in season, he was enthralled. Yet he didn't immediately think, *Why don't I have what she has, since I'm also a believer, a worshipper, and even a prophet?*

Instead, he saw these provisions as a miracle and a sign that Allah (swt) is capable of all things. Zakariyah immediately turned to ask Allah (swt) to bless him with a son. Zakariyah's *du'a* was for something that was also "out of season" for him and his wife. Due to his old age and his wife's barren womb, having a child was seemingly impossible. However, seeing the fruits in Maryam's living quarters prompted his conviction in Allah's power to be reignited. And of course, Allah (swt) responded to his *du'a*:

{So the angels called him while he was standing in prayer in the chamber, "Indeed, Allah gives you good tidings of Yahya..."}. *(Al Imran 3: 39)*

These verses are full of concrete hope in Allah's generosity and mercy. They show me how to respond positively when I see someone with blessings that I don't possess. Prophet Zakariyah didn't dwell on the fruits he saw. He was inspired by them and immediately recognized that nothing is impossible for Allah (swt), no matter how out of reach it may seem.

When we see people who have things we don't have, we can either allow seeds of ingratitude to take hold in our hearts, or we can recognize that these blessings are from the limitless Kingdom of Allah (swt) and use that as motivation to ask of Him alone.

Gratitude is a muscle. It can be exercised and built up, or it can atrophy with disuse and neglect. I have found the following to be a useful guide in building the strength of my gratitude:

- Putting limits on my consumption of other people's lives. Just because their lives are on display doesn't mean it's healthy to constantly be watching.

- Taking the time to develop my own goals and vision. When I am focused on my own development and wellbeing, it becomes less likely that I'll lose myself in other people's achievements and blessings.

- Always turning to Allah (swt) in gratitude and *du'a*, especially whenever I feel overwhelmed by the blessings of others.

- Turning my attention to those who have less than me, then taking concrete steps to offer help.

At the same time, if I'm holding on to my gratitude by employing all of the above steps, but *still* publishing an overly polished and perfected image of myself, then have I done enough to battle the toxicity of the social media world? Just as I care about my social media consumption and how it affects my wellbeing, I should care about not contributing to a system of dishonest displays of grandeur.

If I value honesty, authenticity, and gratitude in what I see and read, then I should practice putting out content that will inspire others to be grateful, authentic, and honest, too.

As an influencer, I take it upon myself to consciously write about my true experiences and not simply offer the world the most sanitized, beautiful version of my life. I don't deny my emotional and spiritual struggles and I am as open about my personal and business-related battles as I possibly can be. I have posted about wanting to give up my writing work when it becomes too hard, about how my past traumas make it hard for me to put my work out into the mainstream, and how single parenthood makes the most basic tasks so much more difficult than they would be for other families.

Many of these things are uncomfortable to put out into the world, but I don't want my readers to feel isolated and alone in their human imperfection. Truthfully, it's the authentic, straight-from-my-heart writing that connects most powerfully with my readers.

We are all on this journey together, for better or worse. We must be the mirrors of one another,[15] holding each other up in love and support and giving away beautiful, good things—the kinds of things that we expect for ourselves.

{The believing men and believing women are allies of one another. They enjoin what is right and forbid what is wrong and establish prayer and give *zakah* and obey Allah and His Messenger. Those— Allah will have mercy upon them. Indeed, Allah is Exalted in Might and Wise.} *(at-Tawbah 9: 71)*

What Allah gives you is always better

One morning as I dropped my daughter off at school, I saw a father and son walking in together, hand in hand. The boy was tiny and couldn't have been older than three and a half. He looked neat and adorable in his crisp uniform, a shiny new backpack slung over his shoulder. I overheard the father encouraging him, saying, "Look at you! *Ma sha' Allah, ma sha' Allah*. You're going to do great at school!" The boy looked at his father, puffed his chest out a little, and grinned.

It was a moment that may have seemed insignificant to other onlookers, but it struck me differently.

During graduations, award ceremonies, and plays, I scan the faces of proud fathers eagerly recording their children's performances. I see children sitting tall on their fathers' shoulders as they walk through the mall. I overhear fathers telling their kids funny stories in parks and restaurants.

Regardless of how much I've stretched my own heart to allow for greater depths of love to flourish, I immediately feel small in these moments. My shoulders are not strong enough to carry my daughter. My hand feels atrophied and weak as I hold hers. Everything I do, no matter how big, feels painfully *not enough*.

The feeling of not being enough is a beast I have yet to conquer.

In mythological stories, heroes often have to battle great beasts in order to survive, rescue someone, or get their hands on some magnificent treasure. They face three-headed beasts, fire-breathing dragons, or shape-shifters that represent their greatest fear. In this story archetype, the heroes are taken to the brink of failure and stare into the gaping mouth of the beast before they try one last blow. Only then do they succeed.

We will all stare into the open mouth of that beast at some point in our lives.

The mother of Prophet Musa (as) feared for his life because Pharaoh had sent an army to kill all the infant boys born to the Children of Israel. She put him in a basket and pushed him into the river, away from the danger that was nearing their doorstep.

This baby didn't drift away into some quiet, distant, safe place. He floated right into the home of Pharaoh himself, right into the home of the very person who wanted him dead! He was inside the mouth of the beast—a beast that had the potential to snap his jaws shut and devour Musa whole.

Allah (swt) protected Musa and, for a time, tamed the beast that was Pharaoh. Even after Musa was saved from being killed, he didn't just live his life in the palace. He was returned to the embrace of his own mother so that

{She might be content and not grieve and that she would know that the promise of Allah is true.} *(al-Qasas 28: 13)*

A mother's greatest fear is losing her child, but it was her trust in God that gave Musa's mother the courage to face that real, tangible fear head on.

My greatest fear was losing my husband. I would worry if he was fifteen minutes late. I became anxious if his phone died and I couldn't get ahold of him. If he had a night shift at the pharmacy where he worked, I would sleep fitfully until he returned.

And then I lost him. My greatest fear came to pass and I was left staring into the dark mouth of my grief. My grief said to me, *I will devour you whole, crunching and grinding and destroying you, until there is nothing left.*

And there were times I believed it.

When I see dads holding their kids, laughing with them, playfully wrestling them to the ground, I cannot help the sadness that creeps into my heart. But I also have to believe that in some way, my life with my daughter will be better than what I had originally planned.

We must be better off now because Allah (swt) doesn't leave the believers to themselves even for the blink of an eye; because He is *al-Wali*, the close Friend and Protector of the believers; because everything He plans for us is to strengthen us and push us to stand up and walk forward with faith and confidence.

When I'm feeling especially alone in this strange world, I remember the incident where Abu Bakr (ra) and the Prophet (saw) were migrating to Madinah and had to hide in a cave so as not to be found by the Quraysh who were trailing them.

At one point, they were nearly found by the search parties. While hiding in a cave, Abu Bakr (ra) anxiously said, "If any of them should look under his feet, he would see us!"

Then Prophet Muhammad (saw) reassured him, saying, "O Abu Bakr! What do you think of two (persons), the third of whom is Allah (swt)?"[16]

The same instance is referred to in the Qur'an, quoting the Prophet's words to Abu Bakr:

{Grieve not: verily, Allah is with us.} *(at-Tawbah 9: 40)*

I have repeated this statement to myself many

times as I hold my daughter's hand: *Allah is with us. Allah is with us. Allah is with us.* It is only through this knowledge that my loneliness cannot own me absolutely. It is only through my belief that Allah (swt) does not abandon the believers that I have been able to face my brokenness head on.

There is a wisdom that we cannot see behind the things, people, and events that Allah (swt) brings into our lives—and even in what He takes away.

In Surat al-Kahf, we are given three beautiful examples of Allah's wisdom. In the story that many of us know, Prophet Musa meets Al-Khidr and they journey together so that Musa may learn from him.

The first thing Al-Khidr does is make a hole in a boat belonging to some fishermen who had agreed to transport the two men on board for free. Then Al-Khidr does what seems unthinkable: he kills a young boy. Lastly, Al-Khidr finds a crumbling wall in a small town and fixes it without asking for payment, even after the people of the town denied them the minimum hospitality.

Prophet Musa is shocked to witness Al-Khidr's actions that seemingly cause damage and pain to those around them (or make no sense at all in the case of the wall). In response to the incident with the young boy, Musa says to Al-Khidr:

{You have certainly done a deplorable thing!} *(al-Kahf 18: 74)*

Later on, Al-Khidr explains to Musa that behind the fishermen was a king forcefully seizing all the boats he came across, and the (repairable) hole would discourage the king from stealing this one. He then explains that the boy's parents were righteous believers, and this son of theirs would have grown up to be someone who gravely transgressed against them and against Allah (swt). In Allah's wisdom, He would instead give them another son who would be a mercy to his parents.

When Musa asserts that they should have at least asked the townspeople for payment to fix the wall, Al-Khidr rebukes him for his lack of patience and explains:

{And as for the wall, it belonged to two orphan boys in the town; and there was under it a treasure belonging to them; and their father was a righteous man, and your Lord intended that they should attain their age of full strength and take out their treasure as a mercy from your Lord. And I did it not of my own accord. That is the interpretation of those (things) over which you could not have patience.} *(al-Kahf 18: 82)*

Their father took care of the commandments of Allah (swt), worshiping none but Him and leading a life of righteousness. Allah (swt), in turn, took care of this man's children even after he was long gone. Had Al-Khidr not come along and fixed the crumbling wall, the orphans' wealth would have been found and then stolen by the townspeople. Allah kept the wealth hidden until it could be unearthed by the boys when they grew into strong men.

This series of events in Surat al-Kahf never ceases to amaze me. The verses put my heart at ease because they remind me that Allah (swt) is looking out for us, steering us in the direction we are meant to go, and always giving us what's best.

The last story in particular is my favourite. When I am struggling to understand how my daughter will be taken care of without her father around, I remember that Allah (swt) sent Al-Khidr to protect the wealth of the orphans because their father was a righteous man.

To the best of what I know and believe about Amr (and Allah knows best), he was a righteous man. So I trust that Allah (swt) will take care of his daughter, too. Even if it sometimes feels as though she has been left at a disadvantage, I banish those thoughts from my mind when I read the story of Al-Khidr.

Allah (swt) will always send someone or something to take care of the believers.

In the interim, patience is the only meaningful remedy for enduring the things we can't understand. The fishermen didn't know the reason their boat was damaged. Even more heartbreaking, the young boy's parents didn't know what the future held for him. It must not have made any "sense" that he was taken from them so soon. When I reflect on these stories, I start to see that sometimes pain in the short term is necessary to bring about something of great benefit. On my most challenging days, I try to remember that what seems like the worst possible thing may actually be the best for me.

Throughout this story, although Musa (as) knew that Al-Khidr was sent with divine knowledge, he still lost his patience and questioned Al-Khidr's actions when they seemed harmful or illogical on the surface. He, too, couldn't understand the wisdom behind certain actions and events until they were explained. Al-Khidr predicted as much, saying to Musa:

{And how can you have patience for what you do not encompass in knowledge?} *(al-Kahf 18: 68)*

When your heart is struggling to accept and understand something painful, you're not alone. It's normal to not understand. While we weren't given access to the divine knowledge that would perfectly explain the wisdom behind our tests, we also have to arrive at a state where we can say: *O Allah, I don't understand this, but I know You have a reason, and I know You're looking out for me.*

Allah (swt) says:

{...Perhaps you dislike a thing and Allah makes therein much good.} *(an-Nisa' 4: 19)*

It was said that Ibn Abbas (ra) used to recite this *du'a*: "O Allah, make me content with what you have provided me, send blessings for me therein, and replace for me every absent thing with something good (or better)."[17]

The face of my beast used to be grief, but it has shape-shifted over the years. The beast is now deviously underhanded, goading me into feeling guilt and pain over what I cannot control. It whispers to me, in a voice that sounds very much like my own, that my child will suffer beyond measure without a father figure and siblings in her life. It flexes its muscles at me when news articles and lecturers unscrupulously spout statistics about the children of single moms being prone to crime, depression, and unhealthy family lives. My beast hisses at me when I take time away from my child to work on my books, take a class, or develop any of my personal goals, saying, *You are already not enough as one parent, and now you're leaving her—again?*

In the greatest act of defiance I can fathom, I live fully in the face of my beast, kicking it to the furthest corners of my mind. My beasts, my fears, and my tests have no power except the power I give them. The only beasts that survive are those I feed and those I allow to roam freely in my mind.

Truthfully, in the places I most feared, I found the greatest treasures of all. The best of treasures came to me in my darkest days of mourning when I forged a connection with my Lord. In those days, I realized how much I needed Allah (swt) to get me through every moment. What better blessing can there be after discovering the tremendous faith that comes with genuinely raising my hands and acknowledging my need for Him?

In Surat Ta-Ha, when Allah (swt) is speaking to Musa, He reminds him that his mother cast him into the river and that Musa drifted into the place that was most feared but was brought out unscathed; and not only unscathed, but protected with the love of Aasiya, in addition to the love of his mother:

{...And I bestowed upon you love from Me that you would be brought up under My eye},

then He says:

{And I have prepared thee for Myself (for service).} *(Ta-Ha 20: 39, 41)*

Allah (swt) chose Musa (as) and was preparing him for his task of prophethood from the moment he was born—guiding him, protecting him, and strengthening him.

Just as Allah (swt) gave Musa the exact experiences that he needed to grow into a strong believer, He will give you the joy, pain, successes, and failures that you specifically need to recognize His Lordship over you. He will give you every tool you need to worship Him in the best manner possible.

Your job is to accept those tools and learn from your experiences.

In a *hadith* reported by Abdullah ibn Abbas (ra), who was just a boy at the time, the Prophet Muhammad (saw) said:

"O young man, I shall teach you some words [of advice]: be mindful of Allah and Allah will protect you. Be mindful of Allah and you will find Him in front of you. If you ask, then ask Allah; and if you seek help, then seek help from Allah..."[18]

In the original Arabic of this *hadith*, the Prophet (saw) uses the phrase, "*ihfadh Allah, yahfadhak*," which literally translates as: "Take care of Allah, and Allah will take care of you." What is meant by this phrase is that we should take care of the commandments Allah (swt) has ordered upon us (such as our prayer, fasting, charity, character, dress code, etc.). We should constantly be mindful of God and make the hereafter a priority in our lives.

Then we get something beautiful in return: a promise from Allah (swt) that He will take care of us in a beautifully holistic way. He will care for our worldly needs, our faith, and our status in the hereafter. He will plan our lives with incredible precision and wisdom.

Allah (swt) not only planned your life for you, but He also *chose* you. He *chose* a specific place and time that you would be born. He *chose* that you would have certain abilities, certain strengths, and certain weaknesses. He *chose* your tests—as difficult as they may be—not so that you may needlessly suffer, but that you may grow as a believer, thrive in your difficulty, and emerge victorious on the Day of Judgment.

Nothing is by chance. Nothing is random.

We can reflect on the question of *Why did Allah choose this specific life for me?* in order to understand His blessings upon us, appreciate the perfection of His planning, and focus on how best we can worship Him considering our specific life circumstances. But we don't waste our time obsessing over the reasons for everything, and we don't indulge in the question of *What if...?*

We trust that even if we're standing inside the mouth of a vicious beast, Allah (swt) will help us defeat it.

So next time you're standing in front of one of your greatest fears, say to it: *Allah is preparing me, through you, for my task ahead.*

And believe it.

Searching for perfection

On a recent family trip, we travelled to Chesapeake Bay in Virginia where my brother had rented a large, private log cabin right on the beach. The cabin was situated on a one-hundred-acre property surrounded by a quiet, thick forest.

The entire wall of the cabin facing the ocean was made of sliding glass doors, giving us an unobstructed view of the water.

When we got there, I took out a pair of binoculars, walked down to the sandy beach, and surveyed the beachfront. It was completely empty. As a longtime hijabi, this privacy was priceless. After nearly twenty years of covering, this was the first time I would be able to fully enjoy the soft ocean breeze.

The ocean was surprisingly warm when I stepped in. When my daughter splashed me, I didn't shiver or tense up. I let my body float in the dense, salty water, listening to the laughter of my family playing around me.

When we finished swimming, my daughter and I walked along the shore. We'd watch the waves gently reaching across the golden sand, leaving it flat and even, erasing our footprints.

Every so often we'd stop and admire the rocks and sea glass littering parts of the beach. I'd pick them up, feel the smooth, marble-like texture between my fingers, marvel at the ferocity of their colour, and then drop them back on the ground.

We discovered long sheets of shed snakeskin hiding between two large boulders. I held the surprisingly soft white and grey snakeskin in my hands, the intricate, diamond-shaped scales still visible on its surface.

I held that snakeskin in my hands, thinking of everything I've had to shed over the years. A snake only sheds its skin once it's ready—once the skin below it has regenerated. But when I had to leave my old life behind, I didn't feel ready. I felt exposed.

After Amr passed away, parts of me fell away and got left behind until it felt like I had lost all that made me *me*. Every day I was afraid of being found out—afraid that people would discover I was a person made up of pieces while everyone around me believed I was whole. Even though I presented myself to the world as a healed, put-together writer and businesswoman, I was internally fragmented, struggling to find footing and to understand my new self. My insides felt like the surface of a mismatched puzzle.

Despite being fragmented in my grief, I grew and began to wonder: What does it mean to be "whole," anyway? Is there really anyone or anything "whole" or perfectly at peace here, on this earth that's filled with hatred and injustice and death? I don't think there can be wholeness until death and pain are no longer a possibility. There can't be wholeness until we take the first step into *jannah*.

Allah (swt) has never once asked me to be whole or perfect. He doesn't need me to pretend I'm fine. Allah (swt) just wants me to come exactly as I am at this very moment. It doesn't matter if I'm broken, rattling, and lost. I just need to stand at His door, acknowledging my pain, my deficiencies, and my utter need of Him.

Who else would a broken person turn to except the One Who heals? Who else would a sinful person turn to except the One Who forgives? Who else would an imperfect person turn to except the One Who is the Owner of perfection?

Our connection with Allah (swt) is not based on being perfect believers; it's based on acknowledging our imperfections and limitations. In a beautiful *duʿa* that sums up this sentiment, Prophet Muhammad (saw) taught us to say:

"O Allah, You are my Lord. There is no god besides You. You created me and I am Your servant, following Your covenant and my promise to You as much as I can. I seek refuge in You from the evil that I have done. Before You I acknowledge Your blessings bestowed upon me and I confess my sins to You. So forgive me, for surely no one can forgive sins except You."

Shaddad ibn Aws (ra) relates that the Prophet (saw) said that the most superior way of asking for forgiveness from Allah is to say the above *du'a*. The Prophet (saw) also emphasized:

"If somebody recites it during the day with firm faith in it and dies on the same day before the evening, he will be from the people of paradise; and if somebody recites it at night with firm faith in it and dies before the morning, he will be from the people of paradise."[19]

This supplication acknowledges our ongoing internal struggle when we say to Allah: *I'm trying my best*, while at the same time saying, *I know I've failed so many times, so forgive me*.

Around the boulders where the snakeskin lay, piles of chipped and broken seashells were strewn about as though purposefully stomped on and left behind. There was a powerful kind of symbolism in all the shards of glass and scattered seashells on the sand. The fragmented, dissimilar pieces had come together to make a new and beautiful mosaic. Walking along that beach with my daughter, I made peace with being in pieces.

I came to terms with having cracks in my armour and with seeing parts of my life get left behind in the past. As difficult as it is to look at the empty spots in my heart where romantic love and joy used to reside, I now have room for renewal and growth. I have space to take my daughter by the hand and walk along the shore, creating new memories that fill my heart with light.

I will gather the disparate and conflicting parts of myself and pull them towards God. Even if I am in pieces, I'll walk towards the hereafter with hope. I will come to Him as I am, without allowing my sins and imperfections to become barriers between Him and me. I will set my sights on His limitless mercy.

He just wants me to hold on a little longer until I meet Him. He just wants me to gather up as many pieces of my broken heart as I can and keep going.

The vacation was exactly what I needed to feel refueled and reenergized. But while we were surrounded by breathtaking views of sunny beaches and wooded forests, so many things that happened on that vacation made me pause and reflect on the nature of our lives.

While swimming with my daughter on that first day, I scraped the entire top of my foot against a sharp piece of driftwood. I limped away and couldn't get back into the water. Later on, I went for a walk and because I'm usually covered from head to toe and therefore not accustomed to wearing it, I forgot to apply sunscreen. I got an extremely painful sunburn that lasted for the rest of the trip.

Another day, I was sitting on the beach watching my family play in the water, foot injury still unhealed. My nephew suddenly screamed because he felt a slimy jellyfish slide against his hand. Everyone ran out of the water and proceeded to spend the rest of the day standing on the shore, looking out for more jellyfish.

The next day, it seemed that the swarm of jellyfish had moved on. But after a short while, it started getting cloudy. Bright strokes of lightning cracked against the grey sky. I sat on the beach, thinking, *This doesn't seem safe*. So I took my phone out and googled "beach lightning safety," and the results all yelled off the page: *Get out of the water immediately*. So again, everyone evacuated the water.

Reflecting on everything that happened on that vacation—both the good and the bad—led me to realize that it was a microcosm of our existence here. No matter how beautiful something appears, there is no absolute perfection in what we experience in this life. Likewise, no matter how *at peace* a person may appear, there is always some turmoil bubbling beneath the surface.

All happiness in this *dunya* is marred by some discomfort, sadness, or fear. It doesn't have to be an immense, life-altering pain; it could just be a loved one being too far away from you to share your happiness. It could be the distant memory of a mistake you wish you could change or hurtful words you wish you could take back. It could be something as simple as having a painful paper cut on your finger. Even if you're experiencing the best day of your life—even if it's your wedding day—that paper cut is still going to sting.

The imperfection of this *dunya* serves a purpose. It reminds us that true perfection is found only in *jannah*.

We are continuously journeying towards stations of happiness in this world—graduating, getting married, going on dream vacations, having children. We think, *I'll definitely be happy once* this *happens or once I accomplish* that. Then, when we actually arrive at that station, there are memories of past sadnesses or fears of future troubles quietly burning within us.

Just as our traumas, our insecurities, and our anxieties can leave us feeling internally fragmented, the world outside our bodies is littered with tests and imperfect experiences.

Every little annoying pang or pain we experience on this journey serves a purpose. The scrapes, the sunburns, and the nostalgia and worry all remind us that this world will never be perfect. It is just a station leading us to our final destination.

The Prophet (saw) once took hold of Abdullah ibn Umar's shoulder and said to him:

"Be in the world as if you were a stranger or a traveller along the path."[20]

Travelling, by its very nature, is often stressful and uncomfortable. There is only one reason you put up with going through airport security, waiting at the gate for hours, or riding on that stuffy airplane. There's only one reason you endure the stiff legs and motion sickness that come with long drives. There's only one reason you would travel from your home to a foreign place, enduring language divides and culture gaps.

That reason is the destination.

When my life isn't going perfectly, I remind myself that *it's not supposed to*. I'm supposed to have tests. I'm going to lose people I love and money I've earned. I'll get sick or become heartbroken. All that shouldn't take me away from Allah—it should bring me closer to understanding that having a perfect life isn't my purpose on this earth. Perfection is my reward with Allah in the hereafter.

There are no poisonous jellyfish in the rivers that flow beneath the gardens of *jannah*. There is no sun that burns your skin or storms that force you indoors. There is no physical or emotional pain. There is just peace, joy, and satisfaction.

There are angels waiting to greet us when we enter paradise, saying:

{Peace be upon you for what you patiently endured. And excellent is the final home.} *(ar-Ra'd 13: 24)*

May Allah (swt) allow us to be among those who have the privilege of hearing this.

Soul mates

In my early twenties, my thoughts around motherhood were clearly laid out. I imagined always having something baking in the oven and snuggling while reading bedtime stories to my child each night. I wanted to be that PTA mom who organized field trips and bake sales and hosted parties at home. I wanted to be the mom who was always on top of her kids' homework and always focused on their education and leadership skills.

When the reality of single parenthood hit me, all the "perfect mom" fantasies I had constructed in my mind disintegrated.

I entered survival mode then and I still haven't graduated from it. Survival mode means I often don't have the emotional energy to do the *regular* stuff, let alone the *extra* stuff.

If outsiders were to look into my life, they'd probably believe that I scrape by on the bare minimum of parenthood. And in a material sense, they wouldn't be far off. My home is often in a state of disarray, with laundry strewn about in haphazard piles, school papers and half-read books scattered all over the dining room table, and dirty dishes piled up in the sink. Our breakfasts, lunches, and dinners consist of whatever is the easiest thing to eat and cook. Our bedtime routine is mostly just me huffing and puffing while trying to get my child to sleep before an ungodly hour.

What an outsider wouldn't see in all the apparent chaos of my life is how being in survival mode has actually transformed me into a mother who is deeply connected with her child.

I was recently sitting with a group of friends and our children were playing together next to us. I looked at the other kids and was struck by a strange thought: any one of these children could have been mine. If I had married someone else, my daughter wouldn't exist. If her conception had been delayed by one month, my child wouldn't be the same person. If any number of factors had been changed, even slightly, Ruqaya wouldn't be here. It would be someone else entirely. Or no one.

But then it dawned on me that all of these factors were exactly as they were supposed to be. Before she was born, my daughter was a soul waiting her turn to enter into this existence. She was a specific soul, meant for a specific body and specific set of parents. She didn't just come into being when she was conceived or when her soul was blown into my womb.

She outdates all of that.

Before any of us inhabited this earth, Allah (swt) created our souls and gathered us together to bear witness to His Oneness. Now we enter and exit this life in turns, in waves, in generations one after the other. Only Allah (swt) knows when each soul He ever created will come and leave, to whom they will be born, and under what circumstances.

When Allah (swt) first created us, He gathered our souls and asked us to bear witness to His Oneness:

{And [mention] when your Lord took from the children of Adam—from their loins—their descendants and made them testify of themselves, [saying to them], "Am I not your Lord?" They said, "Yes, we have testified." [This]—lest you should say on the Day of Resurrection, "Indeed, we were of this unaware."} *(al-A'raf 7: 172)*

In this stage after we were created, after we acknowledged God and testified to His Oneness, our souls met with one another. We had this experience even before we were born—a kind of life in which we gravitated towards others and felt affinity for them. Although we obviously do not consciously remember this phase of our lives, we now connect with the same people in this world as we connected with when we were first created.[21]

Then we are born and we come together in this life, too. Sometimes we are joined together from opposite ends of the earth, against all odds. God guides us to find each other. We share our visions and our goals, we worship God together, we commit to one another, we smile and hold hands, and we work on improving ourselves together. We are soul mates to one another, in a very literal sense of the word.

Our souls connected before, and they connect again here.

Soul mates are not just romantic partners, as pop culture would have us believe. That's far too narrow a definition! They are a full tier of individuals, all brought into our lives as sources of love.

All the people in our lives have been placed next to us for a reason. Allah (swt) chose them with precision, perfection, and purpose. It's easy to look at our relationships with our siblings, children, or friends as haphazard or a matter of chance. But nothing in this world is just "chance."

Even after we die and our bodies are laid to rest in the earth, even after thousands of years or more have passed, even when no living being remembers us anymore, we will come together with our close ones in the afterlife.

Allah (swt) says:

{...Gardens of perpetual residence; they will enter them with whoever were righteous among their fathers, their spouses, and their descendants. And the angels will enter upon them from every gate, [saying], "Peace be upon you for what you patiently endured. And excellent is the final home."} *(ar-Ra'd 13: 23-24)*

They will enter paradise—together.

Think about your relationships with the people you love: your children, your spouse, your siblings, and your close friends. Those relationships don't span only the years you spend on this earth together. They actually span three wholly different phases of existence.

The fact that we can so beautifully connect with our loved ones is nothing short of a sign and miracle from God. It's His will. He kept our love for one another present from the beginning of our existence until the end, when we will be together for eternity, *in sha' Allah*.

When a believer dies, his soul is given to angels who wrap him in beautiful musk-scented shrouds. As the angels ascend the heavens, carrying this soul, he is called by the most beautiful of names and titles.[22] The souls of his loved ones who have passed before him wait by the edge and meet him lovingly, welcoming him with anticipation.[23]

These souls who will wait for you by the edge, who are eager to hear news of you and their other loved ones, are your soul mates. You are connected to them more deeply than you can conceive. Appreciate them while they are here. Hold them in esteem. Try to understand that they are a gift from *al-Wahhab*, the greatest Giver of gifts.

When I reach towards my daughter as she sleeps, resting my hand on her back or shoulder, I feel her body move, almost involuntarily, as though acknowledging my presence while still fully asleep. She turns towards me, coming close to my body, and continues to dream whatever children dream.

A flower turns towards the sun when it feels the star's newly-rising warmth inching across the sky. It exposes its most vulnerable self in order to receive life-giving rays. The two are inextricably bound together: the sun giving away its warmth and the flower absorbing it.

We are our children's whole worlds when they are young. We are their proverbial suns. We light up their paths so they will know how to move forward. We give them comfort and warmth. We wake them up to the possibilities of life.

It sometimes feels like our children are only taking from us, but we also take from them what sustains our hearts: love, meaning, and connection. What they are giving us is much greater than we realize. They give us an opportunity to fulfill a trust from Allah (swt) Himself and an opportunity to be raised in status for our sacrifices as mothers. I have to remind myself that she isn't just a ball of mischief or a set of sticky hands. She isn't just a body that grows or a bundle of skills that develops with age and knowledge.

When I think about my daughter as a *soul* entrusted to my care, I look at her with more compassionate eyes. God gave her to me—this soul specifically, who has been waiting for who knows how long to enter into life. She didn't end up in the arms of a couple in a different country or in a different time period. She waited in queue according to Allah's command, and then she came. He said, "Be," and she was.

When I see her as she truly is—a soul in need of nurturing, a soul that Allah (swt) intended for me, and those around me—I am able to have that extra moment of patience with her. I am able to appreciate the fact that she's a gift and a test and an entire person on her own.

She has a purpose to fulfill on this earth, just as I do. We were brought together by Allah's will: she to give me the joy that only a child can bring to a parent, and I to give her what only a mother can—the love she needs to blossom into a beautiful soul.

Ruqaya and I have already spoken at length about life and death, about school crushes, about sadness and grief, and about our desire to meet each other in *jannah*. There is no topic that's off-limits, so she knows she can ask me anything. She has seen me vulnerable, irritated, and exhausted. I apologize to her when I lose my patience, which is more often than I'd like to admit. I have told her that I am not perfect and that she is entitled to hold me accountable for what I say and do.

Every single day, and in every emotional and physical state, I hold my daughter close and tell her I love her. She has seen the bare bones of who I am when I am so tired from the day's work that I can no longer pretend to be the effortlessly bubbly mom I had once hoped to be. And in that baring of my soul to her, we see and understand one another.

I don't have to be perfect to be the best mother I can be. I don't have to be a good baker or a member of the PTA. I don't have to raise her in a nuclear family, either. Being a good mom begins with acknowledging that Allah (swt) created everything with precision and purpose. No matter my flaws, Allah (swt) knows I am capable of giving my child what she needs. After all, He placed her in my arms.

My child is my soul mate. We are bound together in this life by the will of God, and I hope in the next life, too.

{Indeed, Allah [alone] has knowledge of the Hour and sends down the rain and knows what is in the wombs. And no soul perceives what it will earn tomorrow, and no soul perceives in what land it will die. Indeed, Allah is Knowing and Acquainted.} *(Luqman 31:34)*

Some *du'as* never stop working

"Can we call Baba on the phone?" Ruqaya asked me early one morning. I had barely opened my eyes, the weight of sleep still sitting on my chest. The question seemed to come out of nowhere, but she asked it thoughtfully, as though it had been on her mind for a long time. The question tugged at me, making me sit up to reply.

"No," I said softly. "He doesn't have a phone where he is."

Ruqaya asks about her Baba a lot. The baby version of her knew him. She knew how his hands felt carrying her, she knew what his voice sounded like when he read Qur'an to soothe her before sleep, and she knew what the nape of his neck smelled like when she was resting her head on his shoulder. At just a few months old, she could pick him out of a crowd. She knew he was her Baba.

But now, Ruqaya doesn't know him except from photos and stories. He is a theory to her, an idea, a figure in her life that should be present, but isn't.

She asks about him sometimes. She asks for him. She says she's sad because Baba isn't with her. I answer gently, but firmly, "He's not coming back. He can't. But he loved you and never wanted to leave you. We'll see him again one day, *in sha' Allah*."

I assure her that he loved her more than anything. I assure her that she is still loved by him, even though he can't call her on the phone.

Every time Ruqaya asks about her Baba, I have to turn my heart to stone so that I am not answering her with tear-stained cheeks.

And stone it must remain, until one day she learns the real reason why her Baba isn't here with her anymore, until she learns that someone took his life on purpose without just cause or any semblance of mercy. When that moment arrives, even I won't be able to stop that stone from crumbling.

For now, I let her be happy with the stories of love and play and joy, and I teach her the most important *du'a* she can make for Baba: "My Lord, forgive me and my parents. My Lord have mercy on them as they have brought me up when I was young."[24]

Every night before she sleeps, I remind her to say this, and I remember that these few words connect her to him better than any pictures or stories ever can. I want my daughter to *deepen* her relationship with her deceased father because the connection between them isn't broken—it's only altered.

Our beloved Prophet Muhammad (saw) said:

"When a human being dies, all of his deeds are terminated except for three types: an ongoing charity, knowledge from which others benefit, and a righteous child who makes *du'a* for him."[25]

Our daughter is the seed Amr planted on this earth before passing away, and now she has the ability to grow his record of good deeds each time she utters this *du'a*, implements anything good she has learned from his life, or gives charity on his behalf.

Allah (swt) connects us to our loved ones through the unseen, even though physically we may be worlds apart. When we express our *du'as*, palms open in need and hearts engaged, our *du'as* spread far and wide, unobstructed by the linear structures of space and time. Their effects span generations, reaching places, people, and times we perhaps never intended.

I am reminded of this beautiful mercy of Allah (swt) every time I read the story of Prophet Ibrahim (as), who was commanded by his Lord to do something that was incredibly painful for him: to leave Hajar and their infant son alone in the desert.

But he had enough courage and conviction to put the command of Allah (swt) above his own wishes.

As he walked away, Hajar said to him, "O Ibrahim! Where are you going, leaving us in this valley where there is no person whose company we may enjoy, nor is there anything (to enjoy)?" She repeated that to him many times, but he did not look back at her. Then she asked him, "Has Allah ordered you to do so?" He said, "Yes." She replied, "Then He will not neglect us."[26]

When Ibrahim was leaving them behind, he made a heartfelt *du'a*:

{O our Lord! I have made some of my offspring to dwell in an uncultivable valley by Your Sacred House, our Lord, in order that they may establish prayer. So fill some hearts among men with love towards them, and provide them with fruits so that they may give thanks.} *(Ibrahim 14: 37)*

When I went for hajj, I saw the manifestation of his *du'a* everywhere I stood in Makkah. I saw believers, young and old, praying with their hands raised, tears in their eyes, calling out to their Lord with a desperate kind of love. They circled the same *Ka'bah* that was built by Ibrahim (as) and his son, then prayed behind *maqam Ibrahim*. They drank the *Zamzam* water that Hajar had found gushing in the middle of a desolate desert.

While Prophet Ibrahim (as) was walking away from Hajar and Ismail, he didn't look back and say, "Where are the fruits and provisions I made *du'a* for? Why haven't they arrived yet?"

His *du'a* wasn't uttered absentmindedly after a quick prayer or said only out of habit. It was made in full confidence and reliance. He had the trait that every believer should have when he or she calls out to Allah (swt): patience. He knew that whatever he asked of Allah (swt) would, in time, come to pass.

Allah (swt) says in the Qur'an:

{Man was created of haste…},

and I see that manifested in my own life and in the lives of those around me. We are addicted to instant gratification—we have become accustomed to having resources, knowledge, and opportunities literally at our fingertips.

But Allah (swt) continues by saying:

{I will show you My signs, so do not impatiently urge Me.} *(al-Anbiya' 21: 37)*

We aren't alone in wanting to see results or wanting to know when relief will come to us after difficulty. We aren't the first people to be desperate for change. It happened to the Companions of the Prophet (saw) when they asked him to pray for relief from the persecution they faced at the hands of the pagans in Makkah. He replied by telling them there were believers before them who faced much more difficult trials…

"But you (people) are hasty."[27]

One of the most trying things is *waiting*. Just waiting. Waiting for a phone call about a job you really want, waiting for your heart to heal after it's wounded, waiting to get pregnant after you're married, waiting for your "lucky break" or your business to take off. Whatever it is you're waiting for, the very act of waiting is difficult.

There is self-discipline involved in waiting patiently for a result—a kind of self-discipline that elevates the status of our souls and strengthens us for whatever will come our way in this world.

Prophet Muhammad (saw) said:

"The *du'a* of any worshipper will continue to be responded to as long as he does not ask for a sin or for breaking the ties of kinship, and as long as he is not hasty (that is, as long as he does not become impatient)."[28]

Sometimes, Allah (swt) makes you wait a very long time to see the results of your *du'a* (it took me *six years* of making *du'a* before I was able to go for hajj). But in the time you are waiting, other amazing things are happening to lead up to your *du'a* being answered. When you look back and see how Allah (swt) was guiding you in every single step you took, you will be left in awe.

Sometimes Allah (swt) will grant you something that you forgot you had even asked for, many years later. When you're holding on to that thing or person or feeling or accomplishment, you'll remember it was due only to Allah's permission and acceptance that you were able to have this. That moment of realization is incomparable.

Sometimes Allah (swt) will not give you what

you've asked for, but you will always get something better for you either in this life or in the next (or maybe even both). The rewards of your asking are reserved with Him in a record that never errs, multiplied according to His mercy and generosity.

Sometimes you will never know the results of your *du'a*. They'll manifest in different ways, perhaps reaching across generations and spanning continents, like the *du'a* of Prophet Ibrahim.

Isn't that a beautiful thought?

You quietly utter your *du'as*, palms turned towards the sky, sending them into the collection of an All-Powerful and Wise Lord. The results may scatter, like seeds caught in the wind, searching for a hospitable place to land and grow. Only He knows what will grow.

I say to my daughter when she asks about Baba, "Keep making *du'a* for him."

It's all we can do: keep making *du'a* for everyone and everything we love, then move forward, trusting that the seeds of our prayers have been planted and that Allah (swt) will respond in the most beautiful way.

The lifting of sadness

When my husband was killed, I didn't know what happened to his wedding band. He wasn't wearing it when I visited him for the last time in the hospital morgue. It was a strange thing to care about at such a time, but no one knew what had happened to it. I thought someone must have stolen it after he was shot.

One of Amr's friends who had been with him on the day of the massacre had been holding on to Amr's personal items. His friend handed the items over to me at the *janazah*—Amr's wallet, phone, and keys. Some days later, as I was going through Amr's wallet, I felt an unusual bump where he used to put his coins. I opened up that pocket and found his wedding band. The men who had carried Amr's body after he was shot took all of his possessions and kept them safe for his family. They knew what to put where because there were so many people who had died. They had a system.

I cried when I saw the ring—tears of happiness that it hadn't gotten lost. Perhaps it was a silly thing to cry over, but it reminded me of the day we went to pick out our rings together. My name was engraved inside his ring; his name was engraved inside mine. We weren't married yet so we were shy about everything, reserved in our words. We both loved each other but never quite said so until the day we were married. The day of our wedding, I put his silver ring on his finger and he put my gold ring on mine. It was the start of an indescribable love.

When I found his silver ring hiding away inside his wallet, I put it on my left ring finger, underneath my own gold wedding band. For many years after that, I wore it everywhere I went.

After losing Amr so suddenly, all I wanted to do was hear his voice again, sit next to him, and feel his hand intertwined with mine. But I couldn't do any of those things anymore. Wearing his ring was one of the ways in which I held on to his memory.

I also held on to Amr by continuously asking Allah (swt) to bring him into my dreams. Dreams were the only place I could still access his smile and his voice. Whenever I missed him, I would whisper a *du'a* under my breath and ask for Amr to be a companion to me in my dreams as he used to be a companion to me in this world.

That *du'a* was answered many times.

Sometimes he'd be somewhere in the distance, in the background of my dreams. I would squint hard, looking past the distractions, my hands pulling at an invisible thread that attached him to me, trying to bring him closer. But he'd remain far away. Other times I'd see Amr clearly while I was asleep, his face and smile shining out at me, illuminating my chest with happiness and hope.

And sometimes other people—some who had never even met him—would dream of him...

A while after Amr passed away, I was reading these verses in Surat al-Inshiqaq:

{O man! Verily, you are returning towards your Lord with your deeds and actions, a sure returning, and you will meet. Then as for him who will be given his record in his right hand, He surely will receive an easy reckoning, and will return to his family *masroor* (in joy)!} *(al-Inshiqaq 84: 6-9)*

When I read these verses, I briefly paused and thought about Amr. I silently wondered if he would be amongst those receiving his book in his right hand and finally return to us, his family, with joy in his eyes and celebration in his voice.

I quietly whispered, "O Allah, make him from the people who receive their books in their right hands, and return Amr to us that day," and I continued reading the next verses.

A few days later, I got an e-mail from a friend of mine who said she had dreamt of Amr.

In the dream, she was walking along the streets of Alexandria and she saw Amr walking ahead of her, wearing the same *thobe* that he often wore to prayer. She wanted to go to a *masjid*, so without looking at her or even speaking to her, he flagged down a taxi and told the driver to take them to that *masjid*.

When the taxi arrived at the *masjid*, Amr entered and prayed behind the *imam*. When the prayer was done, Amr went up to the *imam* and recited these same verses:

{Then as for him who will be given his record in his right hand, He surely will receive an easy reckoning, and will return to his family *masroor* (in joy)! But whosoever is given his record behind his back, he will invoke destruction, and he shall enter a blazing fire, and made to taste its burning. Verily, he was among his people in joy! Verily, he thought that he would never return! Yes! Verily, his Lord has been ever beholding him!} *(al-Inshiqaq 7-15)*

Amr and the *imam* sat there, discussing the *tafseer* of these verses amongst themselves.

At the end of her e-mail, my friend wrote, "I don't know what this dream means. Maybe it means something to you."

I finished reading the e-mail, astonished at what had just happened. In that moment, and in many moments after that, I knew that Allah (swt) was listening to the faint whispers of my heart. No one else knew what I had secretly asked Allah (swt), and no one else knew which verses I was reading. But of course Allah (swt) knew. And He knew what comfort this exchange would bring to my heart.

Yes, Amr is gone, and every day without him contains a new struggle. But what if the alternative was that he were still here, enjoying his life with his family and not being aware that there was a reckoning coming? Would I be glad to have him back in my embrace if it meant experiencing just a temporary joy?

Or would I be more content knowing that one day Amr may indeed return to his family permanently, holding a book with his beautiful deeds written in it, held tightly by his right hand?

Surely, I would want the latter for him.

Allah (swt) brought this sense of strange and merciful synergy to my life. My husband was gone, his body buried in the same earth we will all find ourselves in one day. Yet Allah was showing me, again and again, that He knew my pain, that He was listening to my heart and words, and that He would never leave me to fend for myself.

Such is a mercy that only the Creator could have for His servants.

Even though I've seen these beautiful miracles in my life, sometimes before I raise my hands to make a *du'a*, I still think that maybe my *du'as* are too small for Allah (swt), too personal, or too unimportant. I fear that I am being selfish by asking for what concerns only me.

I stop myself each time this thought crosses my mind, because when I believe I should only make *du'a* for big, "meaningful" things, I know I'll miss out on the feeling of being closely connected to Allah (swt) or feeling like He truly cares about me. Allah (swt) shows us miracles and signs in the world around us, but also in the world that exists inside ourselves.

Allah (swt) says:

{We will show them Our signs in the horizons and within themselves until it becomes clear to them that it is the truth. But is it not sufficient concerning your Lord that He is, over all things, a Witness?} *(Fussilat 41: 53)*

It's equally valid to ask for something as "small" as a good dream, or as "big" as *jannah*. Holding back from asking Him for everything, no matter how minuscule it might seem, is counterintuitive. It cuts us off from Him.

Prophet Muhammad (saw) instructed us:

"Let one of you ask his Lord for everything that he needs, even a lace for his shoe if it breaks."[29]

Our asking Him for everything makes us understand that it is Allah (swt) alone who provides us with everything, both big and small.

Everything is from Him.

Some years after Amr passed away, I forgot

our wedding bands on the side of the sink while making *wudoo* and left home without them. In the middle of my errands, my thumb reached for the rings—a familiar habit I had developed—and the rings weren't there.

My empty ring finger looked foreign. The patch of skin underneath the rings was slightly lighter than the rest of my hand. *Ring tan.* In that moment, it dawned on me that even though the physical ring wasn't there, the love in my heart hadn't changed.

The pain had dissipated over time, but the love remained.

I find it fascinating that it can be so—that we can slowly let go of the hurt, but keep holding on to the love. This is a testament to the power of Allah (swt) and a manifestation of His verse:

{Verily with every hardship there is ease.} *(al-Inshirah 94: 6)*

Bit by bit, the hardship is removed, sometimes so slowly that I don't even realize it's being lifted. But the joy of having Amr in my life has never been lifted completely. My connection to him remains present. My admiration of him hasn't waned. This is a gift from the Greatest of gift-givers.

At the same time, bit by bit, the physical remnants of Amr are being removed, too.

Facebook has permanently disabled his personal account. The scent on his shirts that I still have has gone away. The pictures of our wedding are on an external hard drive someplace, collecting dust. All of his cards and IDs have expired. There is no physical trace left of him—none that I can see, anyway.

Allah (swt) says:

{Everyone upon the earth will perish; And there will remain the face of your Lord, Owner of Majesty and Honour.} *(ar-Rahman 55: 26-27)*

Losing someone doesn't happen all at once. First, he's physically gone. Then you forget one or two things about him. Then you forget more. Then you can barely remember what it was like to have him around. As time passes, more and more of him gets lifted and the sadness gets put behind me.

This is how it must be. Everything is forgotten eventually. Everyone is erased.

I don't remember my great-grandparents' names. Soon there will come a time when no one will remember my name or Amr's.

Seeing parts of him, and our life together, being erased is hard. I want to hold on to every little thing and tuck it away in a safe place. I want to wear it on my ring finger and run my thumb over it. I want to remember everything vividly, as though it happened just yesterday.

But I don't have to hold on to the memories that want to slip away, because as long as Allah (swt) remembers Amr and me and our daughter, that's the only thing that matters.

{…The knowledge thereof is with my Lord in a record. My Lord neither errs nor forgets.} *(Ta-Ha 20: 52)*

Sometimes I still wear our wedding bands, but most of the time I don't. I first took them off and left them behind when I was traveling for hajj—I didn't want to lose them. Before this, I used to think I had to wear a physical marker of Amr's love as though to prove that I wouldn't forget him. Being without the rings didn't make me forget, though. Instead, it helped me understand that whatever love I hold on to in my heart is actually what matters.

I will never "move on" as though that chapter of my life never happened. I will never stop feeling the remnants of grief, even if they have dulled and dissolved into the background of my life. I will never dismiss the love I feel for my husband.

But I can move forward, because that's an entirely different thing.

Moving forward means becoming unstuck. It means not allowing my pain to dictate how I live. It means laughing despite the trauma that made me cry for months and years. It means being excited about things in my life despite having felt empty and blank for so long.

I can have my memories. I can struggle with the ways my grief still manifests itself in my life. I can carry my sadness with me like a single bead dangling on a chain around my neck. I can do all these things while being vivaciously alive.

It doesn't have to be one or the other. God doesn't expect me to do only one or the other, so why should anyone else?

Our own Prophet Muhammad (saw) loved Khadijah (ra) until the day he died. He mentioned her, he missed her, he honoured her relatives, and he cried at the sight of her old necklace. He became angry when Aisha (ra) once referred to her in a disrespectful manner.

Was he not patient? He was. He was the epitome of patience.

So let me have my heart the way God created it—to be full of love, to feel the devastation of pain, to cry when I remember a beloved one who has passed away. To do so is so intimately human.

Patience is feeling and experiencing all of these things and continuing to turn to Allah (swt) for guidance and relief. Moving forward doesn't hurt so much when I know He is with me.

Allah (swt) promises us that if we remember Him, He will remember us.[30] So the best thing that remains for me is to repeat the supplication that was taught to us by our beloved Messenger (saw):

"To Allah we belong, and to Him is our return. O Allah, recompense me for my affliction and replace it for me with something better."[31]

May Allah (swt) always remember us and envelop us in His mercy.

{If Allah knows [any] good in your hearts, He will give you [something] better than what was taken from you, and He will forgive you; and Allah is Forgiving and Merciful.} *(al-Anfal 8: 70)*

A place of refuge

All throughout my preparation and journey to Makkah, warring voices in my head viciously asked me, *What if something happens to you here and then your child is left all alone?* The first time I laid my eyes on the *Ka'bah*, though, everything inside me paused. All those voices went quiet.

There are immense structures built around the *Ka'bah* itself: magnificent towering minarets, impeccably designed archways, and tall, round pillars of smooth marble and stone. Yet even in the presence of all this remarkable architecture, the simple brick structure draped in black and gold cloth was the most beautiful and arresting of all. I stood in awe, nearly at a loss for words that I had made it here.

I had come to Makkah with high expectations.

I wanted to find refuge in this sanctuary from the difficulties of the world. I wanted to dispose of the remnants of anger and disappointment that had been piling up in my heart since Amr had passed away. I wanted my sins to be wiped clean so I could return home a brand-new person.

I secretly wondered if, in this place, I'd finally be able to untie the grief hanging around my neck and leave it behind for good.

As much as my heart was moved to be in the *Haram* and as much as my soul was present, I still wrestled with distractions, even while praying with a direct view of the *Ka'bah*! The sound of babies crying, phones ringing, or people coughing would get into my head. The smells of thousands of sweaty bodies praying around me would invade my senses until I couldn't think about anything else. Thoughts of my heat-induced thirst and hunger wandered about in my mind.

I was disappointed in myself. I assumed all these distractions would fall to the wayside when I entered the magnificent *Haram*, but it wasn't that easy.

I was still *me*. The things that distracted me in Canada still distracted me here.

I was quickly realizing that the spiritual escape I sought was not going to suddenly present itself simply because of my physical surroundings. I flew halfway across the world and sat in front of the *Ka'bah* but still brought all my emotional baggage and spiritual faults along with me.

This place—in all its glory, history, and beauty—would not change me if I did not experience an internal paradigm shift.

Allah (swt) says:

{...Indeed, Allah will not change the condition of a people until they change what is in themselves...} *(Ra'd 13: 11)*

On the trip, I made a single, simple choice. I chose to consistently and consciously remind myself why I came here, even if my heart wasn't as engaged as I expected it to be. In my *tawaf* or *sa'ee*, when the exhaustion caused me to drag my feet and forget my *du'as*, I became mindful of the fact that the physical exertion was a part of my worship. I would admit to Allah every so often under my breath, "My Lord, You know why I am here, and what I left behind for You alone, so accept this act of worship, even with its flaws and mistakes."

In my last *sa'ee*, which marked the end of my hajj, I began walking between Safa and Marwa at around one o'clock in the morning. All the exhaustion from the previous days' hajj rites caught up to me as I retraced the steps of Hajar as she desperately ran between the two mountains searching for water for her infant.

I was jostled and pushed by an unending wave of literally hundreds of thousands of people walking and running all around me. Although I was performing this act of worship in a sea of believers,

I was still very much alone. I was reminded of how often I felt isolated in my grief and single parenthood after my husband passed away, despite being surrounding by loved ones.

As I retraced Hajar's steps, I said to Allah, "You know more than anyone how lonely I have felt, and how tired I have been in this struggle of life."

In saying this, I was aware that just as He took care of Hajar and opened up the well of *Zamzam* for her, He also took care of me at every turn and in ways I couldn't even comprehend.

Hajar (ra) was left alone in an uninhabited desert, knowing that all she had was Allah. Her physical exertion and her care for her child is replayed over and over by every pilgrim who visits the *Haram*.

As a single mom struggling to provide the best life for my child, I felt in my bones the immense honour attached to this act being a part of hajj and *'umrah* performed by millions of believers each year. I quietly wondered if the people around me appreciated how monumental this woman's faith must have been and how significant it is that believers are commanded to emulate a single mother's actions until the end of days. What a contrast this is to how poorly single parents are often treated in our communities today!

By the time I was done walking between the mountains seven times, it was almost three a.m. I was more exhausted than I had ever been during the last few days of my hajj rites. The muscles in my legs wanted to give out but my heart hadn't yet had its fill. I snaked my way through the crowd and circled around the immense outer *masjid* structure to make my way back inside. I wanted to lay my eyes on the *Ka'bah* one last time.

I stood in front of the simple building whose foundations had remained in this very place for innumerable generations of believers. I raised my hands and made my final *du'as* for mercy and forgiveness, for my family, for Ruqaya.

Then I left the *Haram* with tears spilling down my cheeks because I didn't know if I would ever return to this blessed place.

As I walked away, putting distance between myself and the *Ka'bah*, I looked around at the massive crowd of believers whom God had brought here from all over the world. Like me, they'd all return to their homes, too. But just because our hajj journeys were coming to a close, that didn't mean our relationship with our Lord was ending. I knew that no matter where in the world we went, if we called on Allah (swt) with sincerity and need and hope, He would always answer us.

In that modest moment of realization, I had found the internal paradigm shift I was seeking.

I knew then that spiritual refuge is not arrived at only in a specific place or under specific circumstances. It is nurtured in an act I can do no matter where I am or what I'm going through. It is found in opening my heart, detaching myself from the distractions of my life, and raising my hands to say to Allah (swt), *I am here and I need You.*

Whether your hands are clasped and you're sitting on an elaborately decorated prayer mat facing the *Ka'bah* itself, or you're busy at work, or running around with your kids, the moment you call out to Allah (swt), you have entered your own personal place of refuge. It's a place where the stresses and pains of this world cannot touch you. It's a place where you know, beyond the shadow of a doubt, that Allah (swt) is listening to you and answering your supplications.

On my way back to Canada, I held on to my newfound understanding that I could enter my own place of refuge whenever I raised my hands to Allah (swt).

If you and I are fortunate enough to find a home there, in that fortified shelter, we have certainly been given the most valuable gift.

God is omnipresent. He does not change or die. He is the Ever-Living. His mercy is a shelter for all those who seek it and a comfort for all those whose hearts are broken.

Allah says:

{And rely upon the Ever-Living who does not die, and exalt with His praise.} *(al-Furqan 25: 58)*

He is *as-Samad*, the Eternal Refuge.

Acknowledgements

I wrote some of these essays a long time ago, but they just didn't make sense when I put them all together. While I was trying to figure out *why* they didn't work, I was blessed to go for hajj. I made *duʿa* for this book there—to gain enough clarity to know how to finish it. Little did I know that it would be my hajj experience itself that would actually complete this book. Allah (swt) knew that, and He took me to where I needed to go.

So, always first: All praise and thanks is due to Allah, Lord of the Worlds.

Thank you to my friend, Hajera, who believed in this book and spent countless hours helping me think through and edit my writing. If it weren't for her, it would still be sitting in a Word document on my computer.

Thank you to my beta readers: Sara Saker, Nobera Chowdhury, Memona Hossain, Asma Ali, and Sumayyah, Mariam, and Nusaybah Hussein. The discussions that followed meant a great deal to me.

Thank you to Noor Syed and Samier Kheirredine for making my hajj trip possible. Thank you to Rania Lawendy, my friend and hajj buddy who forced me to keep going when it got so hard that I just wanted to quit.

Thank you to Sh. Mohammad Elshinawy from Yaqeen Institute who reviewed this text and was always available to help with my questions and confirm the accuracy of my sources.

Thank you to my parents, who have never stopped supporting me.

Thank you to everyone in the world who has come across my writing and sent me a message of love and encouragement. Positive words are transformative in every way.

To my readers who kept asking when *A Place of Refuge* was coming out: Thank you for keeping me on my toes.

May Allah (swt) accept this from all of us.

Glossary of Arabic and Islamic Terms

- *abaya:* a loose outer garment worn by Muslim women
- *alhamdu lillah:* all praise and thanks is due to Allah
- *Allahu akbar:* Allah is Most Great
- *'asr:* the third prayer of the five daily prayers, performed in the late afternoon
- *ayah:* a Qur'anic verse; also means a sign or miracle
- Bayt ul-Maqdis: Masjid al-Aqsa in Jerusalem
- *bismillah:* in the name of Allah
- *du'a:* supplication
- *dunya:* the life of this world
- *fajr:* the first prayer of the day, performed between dawn and sunrise
- *hadith:* a saying or action of Prophet Muhammad (saw) that was narrated and recorded by his Companions and later generations
- *hadith qudsi:* a *hadith* for which the *meaning* is from Allah Himself and the words are related from the Messenger of Allah (saw)
- *Haram:* the Sacred Mosque in Makkah containing the *Ka'bah* and the surrounding areas
- hajj: the pilgrimage to Makkah that all Muslims

are obligated to make one in their lifetime (if they are financially and physically able)

- hijab: clothing prescribed for Muslim women; in this text it refers to the head scarf
- hijabi: a casual term for a woman who observes hijab
- *ihram:* a state of consecration entered into by a Muslim before undertaking hajj or 'umrah; may also refer to the garment worn by men during the state of *ihram*
- *imam:* the leader of the congregational prayers
- *in sha' allah:* God willing
- *'isha:* the fifth and final prayer of the day, performed at night
- *janazah:* the Muslim funeral or funeral prayer
- *jannah:* paradise, heaven
- *Ka'bah:* the cube-shaped building at the center of Masjid al-Haram in Makkah, Saudi Arabia; it is visited by millions of pilgrims each year. Muslims around the world face the *Ka'bah* while performing their daily prayers.
- *ma sha' Allah:* an expression of admiration, appreciation, or surprise; *lit.,* "what God has done"
- *mabrook:* an expression of congratulations, wishing blessings for the recipient
- *maghrib:* the fourth prayer of the day, performed after sunset
- *maqam Ibrahim:* "the station of Ibrahim," behind which pilgrims pray after the conclusion of the *tawaf* of 'umrah or hajj

- *masjid:* mosque
- Al-Masjid Al-Nabawi: the Prophet's Mosque in Madinah
- *meeqat:* a specific boundary point at which a Muslim performing hajj or *'umrah* must enter into the state of *ihram*
- *nasheed:* an Islamic vocal song, often performed *a capella*
- Qur'an: the Islamic sacred book, believed to be the word of Allah as revealed to Muhammad (saw) through Angel Jibreel
- *sa'ee:* walking (and sometimes running) between Safa and Marwa during hajj or *'umrah*; the distance between one hill and the other is covered seven times
- Safa and Marwa: two hills in Masjid al-Haram in Makkah; pilgrims performing hajj or *'umrah* walk between them seven times
- *seerah:* the biography of the Prophet Muhammad (saw)
- *sujood:* prostration with the nose and forehead touching the floor
- *tadabbur:* deep reflection and contemplation, especially on verses and meanings of the Qur'an
- *talbiyah:* a specific prayer voiced by pilgrims during hajj or 'umrah after pronouncing the intention to enter into the state of *ihram*
- *tawaf:* counterclockwise circling of the *Ka'bah* as part of hajj or *'umrah,* performed as seven circuits

- *thobe:* a long, loose garment worn by Muslim men
- *'umrah:* a lesser pilgrimage to Makkah that can be performed at any time during the year
- *wudoo:* the ritual washing or ablution performed before prayer or touching the Qur'an
- *zakah:* obligatory alms based on a percentage of excess wealth, given to the poor and others
- *Zamzam:* a well located in Masjid al-Haram in Makkah; may also refer to the water from this well

Names of Allah appearing in this book
- *al-Fattah*: the Opener
- *as-Samad*: the Eternal Refuge
- *al-Wahhab*, the Bestower of gifts
- *al-Wali*: the close Friend and Protector of the believers

English names of prophets and other figures appearing in this book
- Ibrahim: Abraham
- Ismail: Ishmael
- Maryam: Mary (mother of Jesus)
- Musa: Moses
- Ya'qoub: Jacob
- Yahya: John (the Baptist)
- Yusuf: Joseph
- Zakariyah: Zechariah

Grades of hadith appearing in this book

- *saheeh:* sound; the most authentic level of *hadith*
- *hasan:* reliable; one of the strongest classifications of *hadith*

Endnotes

1   In his *tafseer* for the verse below, al-Qurtubi reported that Umar ibn al-Khattab (ra) heard a man saying, "O Allah, make me among the few." Umar asked, "What is this supplication?" The man said, "I refer to the saying of Allah, the Exalted:
    {And few of my servants are grateful.}" *[Saba 34: 13]*
    Umar said, "All of the people know better than you, O Umar!"

2   Muslim.

3   Bukhari and Muslim. There are two views. One is that it is the hour before the *khutbah* (sermon) on Friday, the other (which is usually considered the more correct) is that it is the last hour before *maghreb*. See https://islamqa.info/en/answers/82609/defining-the-hour-when-duaa-is-answered-on-friday. Accessed March 9, 2020.

4   Anas (ra) reported that the Messenger of Allah (saw) passed by a Bedouin while he was supplicating in his *salah* (obligatory prayer), saying:
    "O the One Whom eyes cannot see, Who cannot be imagined, Who is beyond description, Who

is unaffected by happenings, Who cannot be overwhelmed by the vicissitudes of time, Who knows the weight of the mountains, the volume of the oceans, the number of falling raindrops, the number of leaves on the trees, and everything upon which the night darkens and upon which the day brightens. No sky can hide another from Him, no surface of the earth can hide another from Him, no ocean can hide anything within its depths from Him, and no mountain can conceal from Him anything within its rocks. Make the last part of my life the best, make the best of my deeds the last, and make my best day the one in which I meet You."

Thereafter the Prophet (saw) sent someone to fetch him, saying, "When he finishes praying, bring him to me." When the man finished praying, he was brought to him. The Messenger of Allah (saw) had been given some gold as a gift, so when the Bedouin came he (saw) gave it to him. The Messenger of Allah (saw) said, "O Bedouin, where are you from?" He replied, "From Bani Amir ibn Sa'sa'ah, O Messenger of Allah."

He (saw) asked, "Do you know why I gave you this gold?" The man said, "Because of the lineage between us, O Messenger of Allah." The Prophet (saw) said, "Lineage has its rights, but I gave you this gold because of your wonderful praising of Allah."

(*al-Mu'jam ul-Awsat* of Tabarani, hadith 9448;
al-Haythami said the narrators in this chain are
authentic.)

5 Bukhari, Ahmad, and others.

6 Ibn Hibban in his *Saheeh* and Ibn as-Sunni.
Graded *saheeh* by Ibn Hajar and Abdul-Qadir
al-Arna'out.

7 At-Tabarani, graded *saheeh* by al-Albani.

8 Muslim.

9 Shakir, Omar and Arthur R. and Barbara D.
Finberg, "All According to Plan: The Rab'a
Massacre and Mass Killings of Protesters
in Egypt." Human Rights Watch website.
August 12, 2014. https://www.hrw.org/
report/2014/08/12/all-according-plan/raba-
massacre-and-mass-killings-protesters-egypt.
Accessed March 9, 2020.

10 Ahmad, Abu Dawood, and at-Tirmidhi, who
stated that it is *saheeh*; Ibn Hibban in his
Saheeh; Hakim, who says that it is *saheeh* upon
the conditions of Bukhari and Muslim.

11 Wharnsby, Dawud, "Lullaby." *Road to
Madinah*. Chicago: Sound Vision, 1998.

12 Ahmad, Abu Dawood, and at-Tirmidhi, who
stated that it is *saheeh*. Ibn Hibban in his
Saheeh, Hakim, who says that it is *saheeh* upon
the conditions of Bukhari and Muslim.

13 Miller, Caroline, "Does Social Media Cause Depression?" Child Mind Institute website. https://childmind.org/article/is-social-media-use-causing-depression/. Accessed March 9, 2020.

14 Bukhari and Muslim.

15 Bukhari, *al-Adab al-Mufrad*; graded *hasan* by al-Albani.

16 Bukhari and Muslim.

17 Bukhari, *al-Adab al-Mufrad*.

18 at-Tirmidhi, who graded it *saheeh*.

19 Bukhari.

20 Bukhari.

21 Abu Huraira (ra) reported that the Prophet (saw) said:
"The souls are troops collected together. They come close upon what they recognize, and they differ upon what they reject."
This *hadith* was recorded by Bukhari and Muslim.
For more information on this subject, refer to https://islamqa.info/en/answers/3864/the-meaning-of-the-hadeeth-147souls-are-like-conscripted-soldiers148. Accessed March 12, 2020.

22 Ahmad and Abu Dawood; graded *saheeh* by al-Albani.

23 See https://islamqa.info/en/answers/20820/do-the-dead-visit-or-feel-or-see-one-another-in-their-graves. Accessed March 11, 2020.

24 *Nuh 14: 71* and *al-Isra' 17: 24.*

25 Muslim.

26 Bukhari.

27 Bukhari.

28 Muslim. The latter part of the *hadith* reads: "It was asked, 'O Messenger of Allah, and what does it mean to be hasty?' He responded, 'A worshipper says, "I have prayed and prayed, and I don't see that it will be accepted," so he gives up hope of being answered, and leaves *du'a.*'"

29 at-Tirmidhi, graded *saheeh* by as-Suyooti.

30 *al-Baqarah 2: 152.*

31 Muslim, Abu Dawood, at-Tirmidhi, and Ibn Majah.

References

Miller, Caroline. "Does Social Media Cause Depression?" Child Mind Institute website. https://childmind.org/article/is-social-media-use-causing-depression/. Accessed March 9, 2020.

Saheeh International. *The Qur'an: Arabic Text with Corresponding English Meanings*. Jeddah: Dar Abul-Qasim, 1997.

Shakir, Omar and Arthur R. and Barbara D. Finberg. "All According to Plan: The Rab'a Massacre and Mass Killings of Protesters in Egypt." Human Rights Watch website. August 12, 2014. https://www.hrw.org/report/2014/08/12/all-according-plan/raba-massacre-and-mass-killings-protesters-egypt. Accessed March 9, 2020.

Wharnsby, Dawud. "Lullaby." *Road to Madinah*. Chicago: Sound Vision, 1998.

ASMAA HUSSEIN is an author, entrepreneur, and single mother of an exceptionally opinionated daughter. She is most well known for her book *A Temporary Gift: Reflections on Love, Loss, and Healing* (2015), a memoir of her experiences wrestling with faith and patience after the death of her husband in 2013. In 2015 Asmaa founded Ruqaya's Bookshelf, a publishing company focused on producing children's books featuring strong Muslim characters. You can find her work online at *www.ruqayasbookshelf.com*. She currently lives in Toronto with her daughter, Ruqaya.